The Enchanted Oasis of the Ringed Dove

and Other Sufi Teaching Stories

by
Adnan Sarhan

Sufi Foundation of America
Torreon, NM

© 1994 by Sufi Foundation of America
First Edition

All rights reserved. No part of this book may be reproduced in any form except for brief reviews without the written permission of the publisher.

Published by:
Sufi Foundation of America
P.O. Box 170
Torreon, NM 87061

Cover art by Adnan Sarhan
Edited by Dr. Michelle Peticolas

Library of Congress Catalog Card No.: 93-086351

ISBN: 1-884328-01-6

Printed and bound in the United States of America

Printed on recycled and acid-free papers

About Adnan . . .

Sufi Master Adnan Sarhan is director of the Sufi Foundation of America and a member of five Sufi orders: Qadri, Naqshibandi, Rafai, Mevlevi, and Malamati. Internationally known for the Shattari (Rapid) Method, his work develops higher intelligence and awareness, and causes people to become creative and innovative by destroying all types of bad habits.

Adnan leads participants in a wide range of timeless techniques. Based on various traditions of scholarship, meditative sciences, physical exercise, mystical dance and music, the work signals a connection to the past which stretches back twelve hundred years. Exercises, meditation, drumming, movement, dancing and whirling are used to heighten concentration and produce bodily changes, including slower heart rates, lower blood pressure, and shifts in perception opposite to those caused by stress.

Over the years Adnan has conducted workshops at prestigious institutions throughout the United States and many other countries of the world including: the United Nations in New York, The World Congress of Psychology in Switzerland, The Earth Summit in Brazil and conferences of Humanistic Psychology. Each summer he directs an intensive two-month seminar at the Sufi Foundation Retreat Center in the Manzano Mountains of New Mexico.

For further information about that program, contact:

Sufi Foundation
P.O. Box 170
Torreon, NM 87061
(505) 384-5135

Contents

The Enchanted Oasis of the Ringed Dove 1
   The Dream of the Wish 1
   The Poison of Negative Thought 3
   The Coo-Coo Queen of the Sparrows 4
The Living Magical Reality 7
Your Thought Between Heaven and Hell 10
Ronnie Good Ram 13
   The Wakeful Night of the Sheep 14
   The Moon and the Werewolf 16
   Dr. Goodtooth and the Candy 17
   Ancient Chicken of China 19
   Melanie Garnish, Delight of the Night 21
   The Dream of the Grocer 23
   The Heedless People 26
   Man, the Son of His Habits 28
   The Pleasure of The Spirit 31
What the Foolish Man Says to the Fool 32
The Kangaroo and the Rice Cake 34
   Kung Fu Mouse and the Cat 35
   Feast of the Beautiful Creatures of the Forest 38
   The Rice and Strawberry Shortcake 39
Desires 41
Yes And No 42
High Level of Knowledge 45
   Insensitive Life in a Barrel 46
   Mr. Wisefish and the Grandson of Geronimo 48
   Ice Cream, Pie and the Nerve Pinch 49
   Desiree and the Mystery of the Veil 51
Man and His Thought 53
   The Forgetful State 54
   Man Between Spirit and No Spirit 55
   Man Under Material 57
   Man With a Dead Heart 58

    When the Ego Wears a Thousand Shoes 60
The Cow **62**
    How Cowawi Outwitted the Rancher 63
    The Miraculous Revelation of the Cow 65
    Cowawi's Philosophical Advice to Man 67
    Consciousness and Shallow Thought 69
    The Present is Heaven on Earth 70
    Miss Universe, the Pleasure of the Heart 72
    Baby Ruth 73
    The Gifts of God and Man 75
A Sea of Nectar and Roses **77**
The Crow Who Forgot His Wings **79**
The Best with Good Intention **81**
Anger, the Man and the Donkey **83**
Invitation from Heaven **86**
The Rain **88**
    The Emperor and the Pickled Pig's Knuckles 89
    Two Kinds of Contentment 90
    The Spirit in the Glass 91
    Zakareeyah, Mary and John the Baptist 92
    The Rabbit and the Fountain Pen 93
    When You Get the Attribute of the Wall 94
    The Bird and the Cage 95

The Enchanted Oasis of the Ringed Dove

and Other Sufi Teaching Stories

The Enchanted Oasis of the Ringed Dove

The breath feeds the soul and the breath will take you to heaven. The breath feeds the ego and the breath will take you to hell. It is the thought that is carried on the breath which determines your rise or fall. If your thought is positive, you will be positive and if it is negative, you will be negative.

If you project in your mind, a perfumed rose, with breath to animate the rose in your imagination, you will mentally create an image of a sweet garden. That garden and the sweetness of the rose will help to elevate you to tranquility. Tranquility will help you to be peaceful.

Your thoughts will be peaceful thoughts and you will be in a state of peace. Scatteredness, tension and negativity will disappear. Serenity, pleasant feelings and a mood of delight will become the normal way of life if you wish it to be that way.

The Dream of the Wish

A wish is a tender word and beautiful, but it could be a wishy-washy wish. A wish could stay on the level of a dream and stay there as a dream and be no more than a dream. That is the place of a wishy-washy wish.

Adnan Sarhan

There is another way to look at a wish. And that wish can be a dream that comes true through practical action with determination. The dream of the wish will manifest itself and become part of your reality and the dream will be a living dream. The dream will exist in you and will be with you and become part of you. You will live it and the dream will live you.

So, when the beautiful wish and the lovely dream and you merge together, your life will be a dream which is fulfilled in the moment and will bloom like a rose in a garden in the desert. The rose will breathe the pure breeze and the scent of wild flowers when the desert blossoms with the showers that bring with it the happiness of heaven.

The dream, the wish, the breath and reality are bound in a relationship that is imbedded in the hidden existence. The thought is the key to unlock the secret door. The door with pleasure is open all the way to you when your thought is pure thought, when your thought is beautiful thought, when your thought is happiness that welcomes the bright light of the dawn. Your thought will breathe the crimson rays of the dawn like wine in a goblet of light.

Positive thought is a reality that makes dreams come true. The dreams cease to be dreams as in the state of projection and imagination and become real. The true desire of the heart through action, discipline and the reality, becomes awake and alive, now, in the moment and in the heart of your present. You will be awake and alive in the wakeful, beautiful state of a wakeful human being, living in the heart of time.

You will be in time with the time, feeling the joy, the zest and pleasure of the time when you know the value of the time. Live it in the present before it passes you by and becomes past.

The Enchanted Oasis of the Ringed Dove

Past means gone, finished or dead. When the time passes you in the present, you will have no connection to it and you won't know its value and its beauty and its delight.

The Poison of Negative Thought

All it takes to destroy the present, the time, the beauty of the time and the beauty of pure beauty is exactly one little, puny negative thought. You are transported on the wings of the fastest, most hideous vulture to another reality, a reality of darkness, confusion, misery and holocaust. Your face quickly and without a second thought will look like the face of a scorpion. Your body will be filled with a poison more horrible than the poison of the scorpion.

Take, for example, a man who is a wrestler and fighter who practices all the time to build his body and to make his body powerful like a chunk of iron and solid steel where no knife or sword could even make a scratch on his skin. He is truly Hercules the II.

If this muscle man, or Hercules, or chunk of iron and steel, would look at a negative man with the face of a scorpion, he would be invisibly injected with negative poison more horrible than the poison of a scorpion. This chubby chum champ with the fantastic, magnificent, beautiful body of steel and powerful chunk of nugget iron will change to a chunk of dough.

You must not take what I say literally, but it is a fact that is known in the Middle East, since the time of Sumeria and Babylon, that negative thought, complaining and anger are like invisible poisons that penetrate the mind, the body and the psyche of those who are exposed to a person with these cursed qualities. He will be invisibly injected with that invisible poison and he will become weak, tense and have problems.

A strong body like Chubby Chum Muscle Bound Hercules with the body of nugget iron will get the attributes of nugget dough. He will no longer be Hercules.

The Coo-Coo Queen of the Sparrows

A little baby dove, fragile, tender, soft, playful and cute who is just starting to take flying lessons with her mother will peck on the dough and say to herself, "Oh my heaven! Oh my Mother! Oh my millet! How lovely is this dough! For a dove it is a luxury! I feel dandy, daisy when I dabble, peck and eat this dainty dough.

"But should I keep eating? I will get fat and my wings will not be able to carry me and I will not be able to fly. Besides, I don't know how to fly yet. May God curse this angry and negative man who caused Hercules, with the body of armored iron and steel, to be a body of dough. I keep eating it and I can't stop eating.

"I am getting fat, tense and negative, whereas before I was slender, tender, happy and lucky like a singing nightingale. Everyone loved my coo-cooing when I sang. Even myself, I loved it when I was coo-cooing. I would coo-coo all night and all day on the balcony of my little house on the top of a big, beautiful tree.

All the sparrows would come at dawn to my house, wich-wiching and telling me, 'Please, Dove Dove Dusha, come out from your house and coo-coo-coo for us. We woke up before the dawn and we flew in a hurry to come and listen to you. You are our idol and prima donna. We have all decided to make you our Coo-Coo Queen and we brought you a ring of roses to put around your neck.'

The Enchanted Oasis of the Ringed Dove

"I accepted their offer. They started wich-wiching and clapping their wings in admiration of me to show their pleasure. They all tried coo-cooing like me and I gave them millet, strawberries and cherries. Some of them started dancing by jumping on one foot and then the other, wiggling their tails, turning their heads in circles, clapping their wings, wich-wiching and coo-cooing. It all sounded beautiful and sweet. I was happy and pleased for their show because they wanted to please me. And they called me Dove Dove Dusha, the Coo-Coo Queen of the Sparrows.

Before I ate the dough, and I have quit eating it now, I was on a strawberry and cherry diet. I kept my spirituality and sanity intact, beautifully preserved. I was planning to fly to the Middle East and go to the desert to find the enchanted Oasis of the Ringed Dove. Doves come from all over, near and far, to the magical Oasis of a thousand charms which has streams of pure water running on colorful stones, and black and white sands, and streams of white milk, and streams of golden honey, and date trees with clusters of colorful, perfumed dates — juicy, succulent, tender, rich with the aroma of heaven and the nectar of paradise, protected by the leaves and swaying with the breeze.

The dates and leaves dance playfully, tickled by the warmth of the sun. They smile at the sun, quiver with the light of the sun and reflect its glitter back to the sun. The blue sky envelopes the date trees with the beautiful blue color of peace, purity, dreams and sheer, tender, flowing pleasure of the heart when the heart perceives the depth and endless blue color of heaven that goes to heaven.

The heaven envelopes the date trees with its beautiful turquoise skirt like the veil of a dancer around a bouquet of perfumed roses. The spirit of heaven in that bouquet of roses is always, forever. It is a flux of unfolding reality of magic, moment to moment, never waning, in a motion that generates, creates and recreates now and now and now.

In the Oasis, there are trees filled with strawberries, cherries, figs, mangoes, papayas, bananas, peaches and many other fruits. In the magical, enchanted Oasis of the Ringed Doves, all the doves on the trees sing, rejoice and thank God.

ಬಂಚ

When you do spiritual work for years and years and you do something wrong to others, your spiritual work will be like a child on a merry-go-round. You can't tell the difference between a plastic horse and a gallant, beautiful Arabian horse, sensitive, spirited and blessed by God, which, with a little intuitive sign, will fly between heaven and earth.

The Living Magical Reality

If you see the hidden calm in nature and space or get in contact with it, it will reflect calm on you and will refine your personality. It will purify your heart and gentleness becomes your desire and gaiety enriches your disposition.

When your mind becomes active with thoughts, ideas, anxieties and tension, it will cause a blockage that will not permit you to see the hidden calm in nature and space. The block in the mind and intellect will only permit you to see the form of the calm in nature and space. You will see things as objects without seeing further into the essence or the living force within those objects. The living force is *Al Kayyum*, which means the sustaining power behind the creation and universe, which exists in the moment forever.

When you don't see the essence of an object, it is like seeing a picture of a tree compared to seeing a real tree in nature which moves with the wind and whose leaves sparkle with the sun. The light creates different shades and colors when the leaves and branches sway, dazzled by the harmony and the beautiful rhythm and the tune of the wind, the light and themselves. The space dances with them and around them with intoxication, delight and joy.

To see with the eye of the intellect when the intellect is blurred and not in harmony, is like seeing the picture of the tree. You could say it is a landscape that becomes very still on the paper and its movement has skipped away.

To see with the intellect, when the intellect is in harmony and unity with the intelligence of the heart, makes the seeing like the tree in nature, moving, swaying, dancing, sparkling, living, in romance with the sun, the light, the wind and sipping the breeze and *Al Noor* as pure wine of eternity. *Al Noor* is the flowing light of heaven that fills the heart when the heart is pure.

The picture of the tree on paper is the form and the tree in nature is the living essence in the heart of nature. To see the hidden calm in nature and space, compared to seeing the calm that is not hidden, is like the difference between seeing the living tree in nature and seeing the picture of the tree. Seeing the hidden calm in nature and space is like lifting a veil and you are face to face with charm, beauty and magnificence which cannot be known or perceived until you see it. You become united with it and it becomes part of you and you become part of it. It enhances your mind and your imagination with creativity. It puts you in the moment. You will see and feel the inner love which is abundantly filling the space and beyond the space, a love that has no limit and contains the existence as a whole.

Intellect, reasoning, rationalizing, dogma, religion, rules, the ego and the self all disappear as if they never existed when you see the hidden calm. It is the calm of action, and action, when it is calm, is the cause of creation and the seat of *Al Kayyum*, the sustaining power behind the universe and anything that exists. It is a revelation. When you are ready, it will come dancing to you.

There are two words that are the key to bringing you the power of seeing the hidden calm. If you follow them, you will see marvels and wonders that give you direct

The Enchanted Oasis of the Ringed Dove

knowledge of what is hidden from the people when they are not ready. The Koran says, "You will see what no eyes have ever seen and hear what no ears have ever heard." This could happen if you use the two key words properly. They are "yes" and "no," as simple as that. You have been using these words all your life, but apparently turning the key in the wrong direction.

If you say "yes" to all the things that bring higher positive development, no matter how little they are, and if you say "no" to all the things that bring lower negative development, no matter how little they are, then you will obtain the real thing and you will go inside the reality that is a heaven hidden in the form.

There is nothing in the world, mind, intellect, ideas, thoughts, material gain, relationships, food, drink or parties that can come anywhere close to this complete and perfect experience. It is the inner force and the living magical reality that is hidden inside the simple reality which people are exposed to.

The Koran says, "There is nothing for a man except what he strives for."

ಖಃಛ

If you are negative and confused, you will stay forever negative and confused. No one on the face of the earth can correct this situation, unless you plunge deep in the spirit.

Your Thought Between Heaven and Hell

If your thought is pure, it will lift you to heaven. If your thought is polluted and dirty, you will be in a dirty bar. If your thought is clean, you will be a clean looking person. If your thought is negative, you will be confused forever until you die. You will become the most miserable creature.

A thought that takes place in the intellect of the head is not like a thought that takes place in the heart. The thought in the head relates to matter and things on the outside. All the things on the outside are loose and not connected to lasting perfection or inner contentment.

Thoughts in the head keep shifting, twisting, tumbling and turning over. There is no stillness in them. They create anxiety and attachments that are not positive and cause a drainage to the source of thought and limit the capacity of the mind and intelligence. They bring confusion and disturbance. They burn and waste the energy of the body. They will make you tired, weak and exhausted.

Thought that takes place in the heart never has conflict. It is positive and sure. It is direct and has no apprehension. It is focused and not scattered. You see clarity in it. It is only one thought because it is the right thought. A right thought, when it comes from the depth

The Enchanted Oasis of the Ringed Dove

within you, will be perfect without engendering side thoughts that take you in a zigzagging action within your mind that causes an overwhelming depletion of your power of thought.

When the right and positive thought comes from the depth of the heart, the intelligence of the heart, the being and the spirit, the thought will have a blessing with it that gives you energy, vitality and a joyful flow. You will be content and repose will be your disposition. A negative thought brings confusion, twists your face and brings a look of anxiety to your eyes. It makes you tense and nervous. Your mind and body will be in competition for more misery. Whichever has the upper hand, tension and confusion with depleted energy will be your prize, as long as there is no purity in the mind and body.

If your thought is honey, you will be honey and your face will have a radiant smile. If your thought is sour, you will be sour and your face can't even make a smile. Your face will look like the face of an opossum who has tuberculosis. If a wolf sees him, he will run away to the end of the world and then he will have nightmares.

Any man could be happy by having happy thoughts. Any man could be angry by having angry thoughts. When thought comes from the spirit, you can be sure that spirit does not make mistakes. But to get the right thought you have to get your spirit in good spirits. To get the spirit in a working condition, you might need years and years of the right training, otherwise you will never know what a good thought is, a thought that brings pleasure and contentment.

Mohammed said, "It is your own doing that puts you in paradise or hell. And it looks like destiny, but destiny is in your hand."

An intelligent man digs deep into the existence and pulls out of it the things that makes him content with pleasure. When you are content, the pleasure becomes sweet pleasure and the contentment becomes a container that holds a rejoicing being. The contentment, the pleasure and the rejoicing being pave the way to the spirit. All of these combined, bring evolution and higher development and make life flow as sweetly as a nightingale singing in a garden of roses.

This is exactly what the existence, the intelligence, the consciousness, the creation and God intended for a human being, for what a human being should be like, where every moment in life becomes worthy to be called a moment. Life is the outcome of these moments that are worthy of being a moment of life and life will be a worthy life filled with the joy that is imbedded in the creation.

When a man is stupid, his life will be full of strife and confusion. His thought will be like the thought of a scorpion. No one with common sense gets near a scorpion. Quite often people step on the scorpion with their shoes, but a stupid man steps on a scorpion with bare feet. A stupid man has a magnetic force that attracts all the misery to him. His life is disaster on disaster, forever. He never knows the meaning of joy, contentment or pleasure.

Mohammed said, "Be aware of the imbecile and don't make friends with him, because he will point a finger at you and he works hard and makes mistakes. He wants to do something good for you, but he does something wrong. His silence is better than his talk. His being away is better than his nearness. His death is better than his life."

Ronnie Good Ram

When people of material are lustfully infatuated and enamored with it, their spirit disintegrates and seeps out of them and goes into their car, coat and all the things they're attached to. The car becomes their spirit, the television becomes their altar and the wine becomes the Holy Communion, whether at home, in a restaurant or in a bar. And cocaine is the delight to get them out of their miserable reality.

When Ronnie Good Ram said, "When there is ice cream and cookies, why worry about the spirit? These cookies are divine and this ice cream is heaven." Really, you can't blame Ronnie Good Ram when he runs any hour of the day for ice cream. Otherwise, he would be upset and gloom would put a veil across his face.

His friend Tom Apple would say to him, "What is wrong, Ronnie? Let's go across the street to the coffee shop for apple pie and coffee and your favorite joy and delight, banana split ice cream. Life would be like a dry river without banana split ice cream, but with banana split ice cream, life is like a river. The banana split ice cream is like a boat sailing with the sunset. It is like eating ice cream in a banana boat. It is like a raccoon who found a king's gourmet banquet table when the king had gone out to hunt him but had gotten lost in the forest."

Ronnie Good Ram said, "Oh yeah. Don't talk any more. Let's go quickly. I can't stand it anymore. I like what you said, but action is better than words." And

Ronnie zoomed across the street like a bullet. All the cars started blowing their horns frantically, impulsively, automatically and without thinking while Ronnie zigzagged his way accurately and precisely among all the running cars, just like an agile and powerful ram with twisted and pointy sharp horns like the daggers of the guards of the Queen of Sheba and like a fighter ram in the arena of the Emperor of the Romans eluding the powerful prize fighter bulls who are anxious to thrust their horns in the soft belly of a ram or a man. You might say this is a habit or instinct that the bulls have grown up with since they were baby wooly bullies coupled with the desire of the emperor to make them gladiators with sharp horns.

So when Ronnie said, "When there is ice cream and cookies, why worry about the spirit?" He was absolutely right. For Ronnie grew up in an environment where the real spirit was never known, except that they thought of the spirit as something to do with the football stadium or a ball. They would encourage the players of the football team of the high school by shouting to them, "Go, go, go fight with your spirit!"

The Wakeful Night of the Sheep

Most of the people in the little town where the high school is located do work that is related to sheep. They shear sheep and wear the wool to scare the werewolves, because the werewolves come at night to eat the sheep. There are many of them lurking in the night around the village. All the sheep are nervous and tense and cannot sleep at night, because they are so frightened of the werewolves. When the day comes, they start yawning, tired and sleepy. They will not leave their beds even to go and eat breakfast.

The Enchanted Oasis of the Ringed Dove

Usually their breakfast consists largely of green grass. Occasionally, they trip on a vine of tomatoes or grapes and this is what puts zest in their breakfasts. On the night that follows, they dream of tomato salad and juicy grapes that make them feel exalted, high and romantic, especially when they hear the flute of the shepherd. Sometimes, to the tune of the flute, they do the square dance, but mildly and softly according to the dictates of the tune of the flute.

But as I said before, when the thought of the werewolves is in their heads at night, especially when the howling of the wolves gets very intense, they will be doing the quivering dance all night. Then when they are tired in the morning, they will miss their breakfast and get skinny. This causes great financial loss because a chubby, plump and fat lamb is heavy on the scale.

The mouth of a wolf gets watery from the first sight of a fat lamb. Just like when you say it is love at first sight, especially when the sight of the wolf falls on the rump. But if the sight of the wolf falls on a scrunchy, skinny, weakling lamb, the wolf will be very embarrassed to meet him and he will shy away even if he is on the verge of collapse from hunger.

God knows best what makes the heart of a wolf tick for a fat, plump, juicy lamb that wiggles like a duck. It is really the lamb or the duck that the wolf wants. Nobody knows better than God what makes the heart of a wolf tick. It is a tick for a duck and two ticks for a duck and a lamb.

Because of this, the sheep herders wear the natural wool garb which is taken after skinning the sheep without trimming the legs or the hooves. When they wear it, they have the appearance of the sheep and they go out at night howling, making believe that they are real wolves to scare the werewolves. But the werewolves know better and no garb of sheep will fool or scare them.

The Moon and the Werewolf

One night, a werewolf was lurking in a ditch and he saw these imitation, counterfeit, phony, unreal, impersonated odd creatures, neither sheep, wolves, werewolves nor people. He was basking in the moonlight when the moon was full, swooning at the serenading of an owl song and delightfully enjoying the bats hovering overhead in admiration of the grand opera of the owl.

He was extremely hungry because he had been in hiding for many days. When he saw the counterfeit, impersonated, odd creatures, his appetite was wetted. He jumped from his hiding place and out of his hide and landed on the hide of the counterfeit, odd creatures that he had never encountered before. He thought maybe God was kind to him in sending him these creatures instead of mutton. He was anxious and greedy and he wanted to eat all of them. He was jumping from one to the other, having a chunk or bite from one and his ego telling him, "Go get the other one!"

He kept running from one to the other while the sheep herders were so terrified that they started to do real howling and running away as if the devil was after them. They were all bitten and bruised and got to their homes and locked the door behind them.

In the morning, the people of the village went back to their regular routine of shearing wool and drying meat so they could eat it when the weather got cold. All the people in the farms around the town are sheep herders, so the football team's name was "The Invincible Rams."

Ronnie was a good player on the team and a husky one. He was excited when he heard the people shouting, "Go, go, go fight with your spirit!" He charged like a wild, invincible ram hitting and kicking the ball and mumbling to himself, "I am going to get that ball. I am going to get that spirit." When he ran after the ball, one of the spikes beneath the sole of his boot turned loose and pointed forward just a little ahead of the front of the boot. And when he hit the ball, he blasted it. That is how he got the name Ram Ram. All the people were shouting enthusiastically, "Ronnie is a good ram. Ronnie is a good ram. He is the one who blasted the ball and his feet are sharp like horns."

Ronnie knew what really caused the blast of the ball, but he kept the matter of the spike a secret affair, because the spike was the cause of his exultation and admiration. He turned the spike on his other shoe to point forward so he could hit two balls alternately and blast them consecutively and that increased his stature and magical power.

Dr. Goodtooth and the Candy

All the people voted that Ronnie should go and fight the werewolf. He was afraid to go and face the werewolf, but he couldn't admit it. In the big gathering in the city hall, they made speeches to honor his strength, power and valor and he was in a position where he could not retreat. He stood up on a bench, making a fist of his hands and shaking his arms, shouting, "I am the invincible ram and I am going to break the neck of the werewolf and I will break his teeth.

"And if I can't break his teeth, I will chisel them just like Dr. Goodtooth, the dentist of the town who chiselled my teeth and who said to me, 'You better stop eating candy or I will chisel your teeth to their root where you will not even be able to have a root canal. Your only alternative in that case is to go swim in the Suez Canal and eat canned peaches.'

"By the way and just for the record, Dr. Goodtooth's front tooth is missing. When I went to see him, I looked in the window and I saw him pick up a handful of candy, rush it to his mouth and quickly gobble it down his throat. Later on, after chiselling my teeth, he said to me, 'If you have to eat candies, don't chew them but swallow them like a shark swallowing a fish or like the whale when it swallowed Jonah. Do it perfectly. It is right and valid. It was the command of God for the whale to swallow Jonah. The whale didn't have difficulty in doing so and you should have no difficulty in swallowing candy.'"

All the people were shouting and screaming, "Go, go! Fight that werewolf! Kick him hard! Bite his ear! Chisel his teeth and push him flat on his back."

And Ronnie said, "Show me where he is!"

Everyone shouted, "He is yonder, behind the chicken coop."

An old woman with a broom in her hand shouted, "Yeah! I'll come and help you. Don't you hear the chickens squawking? I'm afraid they will not lay eggs anymore."

Ronnie said, "I'm going to get him now!" He ran in the direction of the chicken coop and everyone ran after him. Behind the chicken coop he saw the werewolf chewing on the neck of a chicken with feathers all over his head. But actually, it was the two wings of the chicken that he fancied as a hat and tied over his head as if he were going to a formal dinner.

Ancient Chicken of China

The old woman with the broom shouted in panic, "Oh! That is my favorite chicken he's eating! My lovely chicken, my prize chicken, my consolation at night and my delight during the day. I love to listen to her clucking and now there is no more cluck. Oh God! What am I going to do without her? My beautiful Chicken Char Chewkeh. She was a gift from Mr. Chin Chick Lin Tick Kick Kick Kick who immigrated from Formosa and brought that chicken when she was a baby. He said, 'She was a holy, rolly, royal chicken who belonged to the Third Dynasty in the year of the Snake, which is the equivalent of 6000 B.C.

'Her ancestors were the property of Emperor Lamb Chank Pinch Wow No No who was a first class scientist, philosopher, theologian, astrologer, an expert in black and white magic and who knew the buried secret under the Wall of China.

'His father put him to study when he was a child with the greatest philosopher and originator of wisdom, calculator of the distances between the stars and the planets and who also painted pictures on water. He was the greatest theosophist of the time. People knew him all over China. He was also known in Babylon. His name was Too Noh Tu Tu. He was the one who taught the son of Emperor Lamb Chank Pinch Wow No No the food formula for the chicken.

'When they eat it, they become as fat as Sumo wrestlers. They are so fat that fifty people could eat one chicken. When they finish, there will still be more meat left: scraps, skin, bones, liver, gizzard, beak, shank and nails. This will be left for dogs, cats, mice, rats, birds, sparrows, flies, ants, insects and raccoons.

'His majesty, Emperor Lamb Chank Pinch Wow No No was the great light of the sun, the strength and the wisdom of heaven, the connection to the center of the earth, the king of the gold and diamonds that chiselled poverty out of China, the bouncer of the wicked desires, the cherisher of all scriptures believed and the original Confucianism, the sharp arrow that finds its favorable spot in the heart of his enemy, especially the barbarians who have no manners, conduct or behavior.

'He was absolutely filled with rage toward people who didn't bow down to old people, especially in the market place. He told the owners of restaurants that it was forbidden to serve a dinner of fat Sumo chicken to the people who didn't bow. The people who didn't bow could have hot dogs. But if they bowed seven times in front of the owner of the restaurant, then they could be served fat Sumo chickens on a bed of rice with tamari sauce. And for dessert they could have fortune cookies.

'When Mr. Chin Chick Lin Tick, who the people called for short "Kick Kick Kick," brought the chicken, the whole purpose behind it was to bring royal blue blood to the chickens of the sheep herders. When they come of age, they have fat bodies similar to the Sumo wrestlers and their bodies are fatter than any pigs you could see around here. You could feast fifty people on one chicken. All my dreams, hopes and expectations have been destroyed now. This was to be the largest chicken producing center and was going to put our little village on the map.'

"Now I have to go and find Mr. Chin Chick Lin Tick. Maybe I have to talk to the congregation to finance his trip to Formosa to bring back another Sumo chicken."

The Enchanted Oasis of the Ringed Dove

When Ronnie Ram Ram saw the werewolf, he panicked and his heart started to jump. But all the people behind him shouted loudly, "Go and get him!" With all the shouting and excitement, and without thinking a second thought, he charged forward, as if on the football field when going after the ball. Before the werewolf lifted up his eyes from the chicken neck that he was eating, Ronnie kicked him alternately on both shins. It was so hard with the spike on the boot that the werewolf doubled over in great shock.

Melanie Garnish, Delight of the Night

The chicken neck flew from his hand, because of the intensity of the hit and the shock and landed in the mouth of the old woman, whose name was Melanie Garnish, Delight of the Night.

Melanie believed that no dinner should ever be eaten without garnish, dill pickle, Worsteshire steak sauce, Heinz 57 Varieties, mayonnaise, relish, mustard, ketchup, horseradish, sweet gherkin pickles, thousand island dressing, blue cheese dressing and ranch style dressing. Without it, the delight of night would be no delight and the night would be dark as far as taste is concerned.

"But if you really want to get the real garnish, you ought to get the Middle Eastern garnish," Melanie said. They are the master of garnishes throughout the history of humanity. Hummus, baba ghanoush and tabouli are real pleasures to make the night a night that comes from heaven. A heavenly night with the real garnish is unlike a night of eating one weenie. For the rest of the night, you will be whining because your stomach thinks that it is not a place for a weenie. The stomach wishes, at least, to have a chicken barbecued on a charcoal fire.

"Anyway, I met a man from Baghdad who knew all about garnishes. I became a very good friend of his and he gave me a clay jar just like the one the thieves of the Ali Baba story hid in. It was filled with many kinds of cucumbers which are only found in the Middle East, also green peppers, chili peppers, cloves of garlic, cauliflower and many other kinds of vegetables. The jar was filled with date vinegar which is the strongest and finest vinegar and only exists in Baghdad. The top of the jar was sealed for two years and kept in a dark cellar.

"When I opened it, I fainted because of the potency and the strength of the conglomeration in the jar. After that, the Middle Eastern garnishes became an important part of my gourmet dinners to make my night the most beautiful night. To make things more complete, I started learning belly dance and I went deep into the mysterious Arabic music. Oh boy, this is the life! Those who choose to die in their offices may do so at their own discretion. But me, never, never! I have found the real things in life!"

Melanie Garnish Delight of Night was screaming with her mouth widely open. She got a shock and involuntarily sunk her teeth into the neck of the chicken. The blood sprayed on her lips, nose and chin and she pulled the neck out with her hands shouting, "Oh my God! Help me! My lovely Chicken Char Chewkeh, I did not mean to bite you! If I had known you would be jumping into my mouth, I would have worn a mask. You are the only chicken in the world for me, my holy rolly baby. You waddle like a duck when you walk. I love to watch you walk and wiggle when you jump up and down. And I giggle when I see you jump up and down. I guess it's a trick you learned in China that no chicken here ever thought of. After you, life will be a disaster unless Mr.

The Enchanted Oasis of the Ringed Dove

Chin Chick Lin Tick goes to Formosa to bring your sister or cousin."

So when the werewolf got hit, he was terrified and shaken. He was crying, screaming, running and shouting, "Oh! I've had it! I'll never come back here anymore." And he ran away, disappearing into the dark.

All the people felt the joy of victory, just as if they were in the stadium. They carried Ronnie Ram Ram on their shoulders, singing, "Ronnie Ram Ram Ram Ram! Fight, fight! Kick his shin! Push 'em back! Push 'em back! Way Back! Ronnie Ram Ram Ram Ram! We will give you all the ram! We will give you all the ram!"

That night, they had a feast of chicken and lamb chops barbecued on a charcoal fire and an appetizer made of chicken gizzard and liver mixed with wild cherries, mashed potatoes with a lot of ghee and baco bits, boiled tripe from the pig with lots of curry and pickled pig's knuckles.

Then they had homemade apple pie with ice cream, coffee, Coke, wine, RC cola and whiskey to top it all off and a square dance to make the event complete. That night, everyone went to bed with happy dreams, wishing to have a feast like that every night. Ronnie was the happiest of all, especially after having been presented with the key to the small grocery store adjacent to the city hall. He could go there any time, day or night, to eat his fill to his heart's contentment — all the chocolate and candy and all the soft drinks — but no more than two cans of beer a day.

The Dream of the Grocer

Mr. Warm Nickel was the name of the grocery store owner. He got that name by having a bunch of nickels in his hand and juggling them constantly to keep them warm. He firmly believed that to keep the nickels warm in his hand brought good fortune. If they got cold, he thought it would be a bad omen and that he might lose his business.

He was working toward making his grocery the world's largest grocery. He was hoping this would happen in fifty years, so he worked day and night to achieve this goal. When it happens, Mr. Warm Nickel firmly and resolutely and willingly made up his mind to take two weeks vacation. But the thought of two weeks vacation away from the grocery was not an appealing prospect because he thought that there would be no other person in the world who could handle the packages or the register.

Apparently Mr. Warm Nickel was unaware that there were groceries and food stores and so on since the time of Moses and Jesus. What he really needed was to go to Sunday school so that he might gain some understanding.

When Mr. Warm Nickel thought about the two weeks vacation, after he establishes his world's largest grocery, he kept thinking all night and couldn't rest. He jumped up from his sleep saying to himself, "Two weeks vacation is unbearable and unthinkable. Just imagine how much money I will be losing! If I have to go away, I'll have to pay for transportation for the bus, train or plane! I'll have to pay rent for where I'll be staying! I would have to pay for food. This is unthinkable! Because of the grocery store, I can eat at wholesale prices because I buy things in bulk. And most of the time, I eat food just before it perishes so I don't have to throw it away."

Eventually he made up his mind to have a one week vacation. It would be the first vacation in his life. Of course, it would not happen for fifty years after those

The Enchanted Oasis of the Ringed Dove

nights of tribulation in making up his mind about how long his vacation should be.

He decided one week was sufficient and said to himself, "Oh boy, won't that be wonderful to catch a fish and eat it without paying for it? That would be great. I know that God loves me because I am a good man. If God helps me catch another free fish, after I've had my vacation, I will bring the fish to the grocery and sell it and put the money from the fish into a new bank account and use it toward another World's Largest Grocery Store."

The doctor told Mr. Warm Nickel that he should lose sixty pounds because his heart is deteriorating steadily. His stomach is going to have a hole in it which will be like a window, open on the north side of the tummy. And the ulcer in the tummy is going from bad to worse. His sensory system is warped out. Also, he has a case of acute diabetes and cancer of the liver which already ate half of it. And he has a tumor in the brain which could spread all over the brain and is getting almost to the danger point that could cause collapse leading to paralysis of the arms and legs.

There were many, many other chronic ailments and diseases that the doctor preferred not to tell him about because they might cause a big shock which could cause a complete loss of his equilibrium. Then he would not be able to work anymore. It is better to keep him hanging on the rope, pretending to hold onto the tail of the fish that he will catch when the week of vacation time comes in fifty years.

It is a true challenge to Mr. Warm Nickel to have one hand filled with warm nickels and the other with the imaginary tail of the fish in his hopeful dream of slippery scales.

Mr. Warm Nickel is but one of millions and millions of people who have grown up in a materialistic way of life which is divested of wisdom, perception, understanding and awareness and completely void of consciousness and spirit. They have mistaken the relative for the real and ignorance for knowledge and confusion for harmony.

The Heedless People

They do everything wrong believing that they are doing right. They work all their life, they suffer and complain, but they are incapable of finding the right way of living. They grow like wild weeds and strangle the joy of heaven and turn the beauty on earth to striking ugliness. They never understand the meaning of harmony, peace and joy. Their life is toil and sweat.

God said in the Koran, "God will lead the heedless to be straight."

A man is a creature of habit and condition. He starts his life with habits and finishes his life with habits. In between the first habit and the last habit, a chain of habits link to each other like a chain of steel that is wrapped around the man. And it is difficult to break out of it. Truly, for some men it is easier to break through the Great Wall of China than to break out of their habits.

The most effective and perfect remedy for destroying conditioning and habits is by going to the spirit. Of course, for many people if you say 'spirit,' they think it is nonsense. You cannot blame these people because they are in the state of *jehaleh,* which means ignorance. The only way to encounter and destroy *jehaleh* is by the knowledge of *ma'arifa,* which means the wisdom of knowing the self.

When you know the self, you will be able to know the real, the pure reality that cannot be known when you

The Enchanted Oasis of the Ringed Dove

are under the command of the intellect because intellect goes up and down like a merry-go-round. And you are no more than a child on the back of a toy horse. The child will never exchange the toy horse for a real, pure, beautiful Arabian horse that could take flight at a wink of the eye of his master and fly between heaven and earth like a magical flying carpet.

So people with the intellect will never go beyond the plastic toy horse and the merry-go-round with all their speculation, hypothesis, theory and understanding. With all the knowledge they get in school and colleges, they could have one thousand and one doctorate degrees, but they are still in a state of *jehaleh*, or ignorance. That is why their faces are twisted and their eyes are dim and their voices quiver and they are always unsure about what they are doing or what is going on. It is true they master computers, technology, office work and shuffling papers, until the papers come from their ears, while they passionately await their coffee break. They accomplish all this with machines because they are machines and machines attract machines, just as spirit attracts spirit and as drunk men attract drunk men, from the first sight.

The intellect is commanded by the ego and the negative self. There is nothing positive, good, decent or respectful when it comes to the ego and the negative self. Mohammed said, "Your negative self is your worst enemy."

Your real challenge is to conquer that worst enemy within you. If you conquer the negative self within you, you will have no fear and no enemy whatsoever on the outside. You will be protected by the shield of God and by the wisdom of God. Your life will be fun and delightful. The birds will sing for you and the rabbit will wink at you.

God created life as a sea of harmony — tender, gentle, soft, bright and it flows from heaven to heaven. The breeze is your guide to the magnificent existence in the real reality which is hidden beneath the obvious simple reality, which is the shadow or the form of the hidden magical beautiful existence, which cannot be comprehended by the *jehaleh* people, the ignorant.

When you find that inner power of the inner reality, you will be liberated from habits, conditions, ego, whims, desires, confusion, greediness, anger and corruption. You will need no artificial means to bring contentment and pleasure, like cigarettes, drugs, liquor and coffee. These are only the tools or the toys to bring fake contentment and pleasure to the people of jehaleh, with all their sophistication.

Man, the Son of His Habits

A man is the son of his habit. A man is an immature child that cannot distinguish between good and bad, wrong and right. If he is not taught the correct and appropriate way, he will grow up to be confused and without harmony within himself or with the reality related to himself, to nature or to the existence. He becomes a wrong person. A wrong person will never know the right and the true reality, which seems vague and nonexistent, because with his limited capacity, he cannot comprehend who he is. He is not connected to himself, the positive self, or the truthful self.

The truthful self is connected with the light of the true reality. The negative self, also known as the commanding self, takes orders from the ego. The ego is wicked and weak and lives in disturbance, thrives in confusion, takes delight in misery. Destruction is its ultimate goal. The ego will lead people to suicide on their final journey of psychological holocaust.

When you use your mind wrongly, you become a wrong person. And when you repeat the wrong things again and again, you become an ugly person. When you become ugly again and again, you become a deranged person.

When a man is the son of his habits, the habit is as a father. But this father does not believe in kindness, gentleness or affection because the habit is a tool in the hand of the ego. The ego has no brain or reasoning, understanding or wisdom and never knows happiness, joy or pleasure. The ego is filled with greed, selfishness, anger, suspicion, hate, revenge, madness, lust, corruption, envy, wickedness, darkness, jealousy, evil, misery, deceit and deception, horror and terror, pretension and vanity, viciousness and complete degenerated ignorance.

The habit is the spoiled and pampered son of the ego and the man is the son of the habit. This father, Mr. Habit, persistently teaches his son, the man, to be corrupt and to take courses in all the above-mentioned titles and to graduate with honors and straight A's under the tutelage of the habit and the ego. When he graduates, he will be a man without anything decent left in him. And he will be called anything but a man.

A modern man in this modern society cultivates his outer aspects and completely neglects his inner aspects. Inwardly, he regresses as far as he outwardly progresses. The distance becomes very far between his outer progress and his inner regression.

A man is a stranger to himself on earth and regardless of how much he progresses with material and technology. Even if he went to the moon, he will still be a stranger to himself in that environment more than he is to himself on earth. He is a stranger to himself on earth in spite of the air, the water, the planets, the carrots and cucumbers, the ice cream and the lemon meringue. Even with all of these things, he can't find himself. So what will he do on the moon where none of these exists? This is a lesson for him to learn to appreciate the breath and to discover who he is.

Life with spirit has the nectar of paradise and life with the ego has the poison of hell. Life with spirit is like a butterfly dancing among perfumed roses. Life with the ego is like a scorpion among snakes.

People of material never comprehend the meaning of spirit because the material creates a thick, cement wall between them and the spirit. The only pleasure and contentment they have is to sit next to the cement wall and gorge themselves on all kinds of drinks that make them into zombies and junk food that poisons them.

They become creatures, neither human being nor animal. The best description of them is that they are disgusting human beings and that is because they are disgusted with themselves. Weak people are wicked people and wicked people are weak people. Greed is their connection to a miserable reality as long as they live.

The irony of the situation is that they are in the lowest and worst state of existence, but they think they are charming, pleasurable, refined and on top of the world.

Truly, the people who do the Watusi dance are more highly evolved in a civil way that is natural and comes from the heart and keeps them attuned to reality, justice and truth. The dictates of the heart are more in accord with the command of God than with the dictates of the intellect that come from a junky, mechanical mind that is the shame of humanity.

The Enchanted Oasis of the Ringed Dove

Mohammed said, "A day that passes without learning about the self is a wasted day."

The Pleasure of The Spirit

Make your thoughts like tender harp music that brings pleasure to the ones who hear it and the heart will dance to its tune.

A thought that originates in spirit knows nothing but joy, tranquility and pleasure. Spirit is the fountain of pleasure. And the pleasure of spirit has nothing in the world that is equal to it or comes anywhere near it.

The pleasure of spirit is imbedded as a trust in the origin of existence and in the heart of man, when the man is awake to the true reality.

The true reality is not too far around the corner, when the eyes are open. Then you will see the candy store but with candy that is unknown to the people, its base is aged in wine and honey that is the best of spirit.

What the Foolish Man Says to the Fool

The ego has the same intelligence as a donkey and the same anger as a rabid dog. The intelligence of a donkey never gets the donkey anywhere except to carry loads. If you follow the intelligence of the ego, your real intelligence becomes equal to the intelligence of the donkey. If you are in a society of men and women, all of them will think that you are a donkey. They will pull away from you because in their super consciousness, they feel you are different from them and that your intelligence is the intelligence of a donkey. Therefore you are a donkey in the image of man.

They have the right to stay away from you, unless they are in the same predicament and their egos have the intelligence of a donkey. Then you are in the same boat. A foolish man says to a fool, "Bring the onion and let us plant it in the snow." What will come or not come is the fortune of the fools. Men do not like the company of a donkey unless they are donkey drivers.

A man with the intelligence of a donkey or the intelligence of the ego is not worth a copper penny. To stay away from him is recommended by Moses, Jesus and Mohammed. But a man with real intelligence will be the charm of creation and God is charmed by him. His worth and value is higher than all the treasures of the earth.

The Enchanted Oasis of the Ringed Dove

And his friendship is recommended by Moses, Jesus and Mohammed.

There is an interesting story told by a great Master, Mohammed Ibn ben Ulyan. He said, "One day I was walking and something like a young fox jumped out of my mouth." God caused him to know that this was his ego. He trod on it, but it became bigger and bigger with every kick and blow. "How come you become bigger and bigger?" The ego said, "I was created perverse. What is pain to others is pleasure to me and their pleasure is my pain."

Ego is the climax of the animal self within you. If you pamper the animal self, and that is the donkey, he will kick you in the stomach and rebel against you.

The animal self within human beings is viciously lustful, greedy, selfish and base. While the animals on the outside are natural, sweet and gentle.

The great Master Junaid of Baghdad said, "Ecstasy destroys the ego."

৪০০৪

Life is rich, beautiful and sweet like honey when the spirit is alive within it. Life is dreary, miserable and boring when the spirit is not part of it.

The Kangaroo and the Rice Cake

Baby Kangaroo Karkaroo Rara Roo boisterously shouted to his mother saying, "I love candy! I love candy and I hate rice cake!" And little Rabbit Bitrab Rab Rab jumped up from behind a rock, sneezed, wiggled his tail and impishly teasing said, "But your mother knows what is good for you. After all, a cake is a cake whether it is made of strawberry or rice. Both are called cake, so eat your rice cake, be quiet and enjoy it.

"Just think how sweet the word cake is and how cake is pleasure-giving to your tongue and how it is a soothing delight to your throat and how your brain tends to stillness like the stillness of the night in a little village on a quiet mountain with white snow which allows no other color to compete with its whiteness. Just think how your spirit rejoices with every bite of a satisfactory chunk-crunch from a strawberry short cake, when the strawberry, the cream, the chocolate, the crust and the topping crumble between the teeth. And you say 'Oh, thank you God for giving me this fancy, fantastic, fantasy of far out imagination.' It is better to have a creative imagination than to be dumb and stupid without imagination, when eating rice cake. So think strawberries, then the rice cake will taste heavenly.'

"So, Kangaroo Karkaroo RaRa Roo, chew your rice cake and keep your imagination going. You will not

The Enchanted Oasis of the Ringed Dove

know the difference. The imagination and the rice cake in your mouth will mix together and you will have the taste of strawberry short cake from paradise. But it is a little better than the real strawberry short cake, because it is known by alchemical masters and through alchemy techniques that you can change dirt to gold. So it should be real easy to change rice cakes to strawberry short cake. So don't worry.

"But, if this technique does not work for you and you still are attached or having a fit for strawberry short cake, you could put butter and strawberry jam on the rice cake and eat it. This will make things better. But keep your imagination going. You can't take chances. Every little bit helps.

"I assure you that strawberry jam will do the trick and you will never know the difference, especially when the jam jams your mouth and your tongue will not know where to turn. It will tangle and mingle with the butter, the jam, the crumbling rice cake crumbs and your face will crumple. With each crunch you will lose your reasoning. Your tongue will do the tango with the rice cake and you will have no choice but to say, 'Oh my God, I love it! I love it!'

"So eat your rice cake with the butter and strawberry, giggle and say, 'I love strawberry rice cake and I hate candy.'"

A mouse nearby heard what was going on and said, "Nonsense. Candy is good, especially after eating cheese. It is an excellent dessert."

Kung Fu Mouse and the Cat

A cat chewing on grass heard what the mouse said and shouted, "You just wait there, let me finish my salad and I will come to eat you. You are my main dish and I have plans for a barbecue dinner, because my whims and desires fancy mouse barbecue. And you are the only one for me. Oh boy, just let me finish my salad."

The cat said to Raccoon RaCoCo, "Raccoon RaCoCo, come and help me catch that fat mouse. I don't feel good. I hurt my toe. I stepped on a nail. And bring some catsup. Catsup makes food taste better especially on barbecue.

Raccoon RaCoCo doggedly said, "I am not coming and you go get your own catsup. When you run, may God cause the pinch on your toe to be of great aggravation and lead you to bad consequences which will take you to a bed in the cat hospital where they will give you bad and bitter medicine.

"I love this little Mouse Mus Mus. He dances for me and he winks his eyes for me one by one. He shows me his teeth, a habit of his, when he is pleased. I love him. You better go eat a hot dog or a dog or I will scratch your pretty nose and I will pull your teeth with pliers."

Mus Mus said, "Thank you RaCoCo. This cat is a savage barbarian. He is uncivilized with bad conduct and no manners. He doesn't know that I have been studying Kung Fu and fencing with Master Mouse Wong Kong from Hong Kong, who beat King Kong and made him run climbing a tree. From the top of the tree, he asked for peace, friendship and coexistence.

"When Master Mouse Wong Kong shouted his war cry, kicked and hit with his hand using his hand as a sword, he cut off the ear of King Kong and immediately swallowed it. It was as quick as if nothing happened at all. The creatures who were watching the fight wondered when, how and where the ear disappeared. I was the only one who knew what happened to the ear. Master Mouse Wong Kong was swift in snitching things

The Enchanted Oasis of the Ringed Dove

at the speed of lightening. King Kong ran like a baby monkey screaming, "Oh my God, I lost my ear. Now I have to have an ear transplant and I wonder who will donate an ear. He is too much for me, too fast and I can't tackle him.' That is why he asked for peace and friendship and coexistent.

"I am gallant Mouse Mus Mus, who could cut a chubby shark into two halves. So let this cat come, I swear by the God of mice, the French King Cheese Camembert, the hot item in the European common market, who all the mice adore, venerate and worship. They eat the last pieces and lick the crumbs on the ground. When they devour all the cheese, they need not sweep the floor because the tongue is sharper than a broom. The cleanliness of the ground is the highest homage to the God of the mice, the French King Cheese Camembert. The Mouse Marmuush, the high priest said, 'Your God is Camembert, a good, goody. Eat your goody and feel at peace with yourself as the scriptures say.'

"I am deadly serious about that cat. If he comes, I will chop his tail with my sword and I will broil it in the oven and make of it cat tail hot dog. I will invite Raccoon RaCoCo for a hot dinner of hot cat tail hot dog on a bed of hot Indian red, curried rice with a lot, a lot of hot spice. Hot, hot, hot! Dinner tastes best when it is hot. Oh boy, I feel hungry already."

Mouse Mus Mus said to Raccoon RaCoCo, "Oh CoCo, you are my best friend in this world. I wish that you were a mouse. Then I could take you with me to the Mousedom Temple to listen to Mouse Priest Marmuush's high caliber knowledge. Priest Marmuush said no one is permitted to the meeting or in the Mousedom temple except mice."

Raccoon said, "Thank you for your concern and benevolence. I am also studying knowledge in the Raccoon Free Thinkers Society."

The mouse said, "That is nice. But I will tell you what Marmuush said the last time he was preaching. He said, 'The space is space and in it is light on light forever. In the space is the earth and the earth is dense. You are on earth at the borderline between space and earth, between the light in space and the density of earth. If you seek the light, you will be light. If you seek density, you will be dense.'"

The cat was not able to catch the mouse because of the handicap of his toe. So, the mouse did not resort to his violent fight with the cat or use his artful Kung Fu technique.

Feast of the Beautiful Creatures of the Forest

He invited Raccoon RaCoCo, who he called CoCo for short and for affection and they had a simple, pleasant dinner on the patio of the mouse house which was on the side of the river bank with a green yard and pygmy bonsai trees which Mouse Mus Mus obtained from his Master Mouse Wong Kong, the greatest fighter from Hong Kong, the winner of the greatest battle on earth between him and King Kong, the wild beast of the bushes.

While the Raccoon and the Mouse were talking, Kangaroo Karkaroo RaRa Roo came by. The mouse welcomed him saying, "Hi Karkaroo, long time no see. What is your pleasure, Coke or Seven-up?"

Karkaroo said, "Oh thanks, I am on a diet. I will take diet CCRKUJ."

Mus Mus said, "What is that?"

Karkaroo said, "This is the best drink that ever came out of Sydney, Australia. It is the elixir of enlightenment and I brought a case of it for you."

While they were talking, Rabbit Bitrab Rab Rab dropped by. He had just finished hiking in the mountain and everyone shouted, "Hi! Bitrab Rab Rab! We are glad you came."

The Rice and Strawberry Shortcake

After the formality, the rabbit said to Kangaroo Karkaroo RaRa Roo, "Tell me about the rice cakes. Did you try the formula for the alchemy of happiness? That is, to change a rice cake to a strawberry shortcake or dirt to gold."

Kangaroo Karkaroo RaRa Roo said, "Rabbit Bitrab Rab Rab, I heard what you said, but I am afraid that I have no such imagination. I don't know anything about alchemy techniques. I am still in the first grade. But I know that I don't like rice cakes. I know for sure that the word 'cake' was put after the word 'rice' to make the rice sound good. But that will do no justice to the cake. For the rice will get elevated by it and become airy with a feeling of boasting and bragging. Because if they called the rice cake 'rice fiber' or 'rice patty' or 'dry rice' or 'cardboard rice' or 'carton rice,' I think no one would ever buy it. It must be someone with a shrewd mind who used the word cake and played a psychic game on the people so they keep eating rice cakes for breakfast, for lunch, for dinner, for midnight snack and anytime they feel like it.

"The word cake makes the people indifferent and unaware of the rice. Actually, they think they are eating cake. I know I don't like rice cakes but there are some great advantages that come from eating them. They will kill the appetite. There is no feeling of pleasure or joy in eating a rice cake. It makes eating a chore. It will stick on your lips like glue. When you pull it, it will pull your lips away from your mouth just like elastic. When you let it go, the rice will bounce back into your mouth like a sling shot. If you eat it with other food, you lose the desire for the other food.

"If you have rice cakes with tahini and eat grapes with it, you will lose the desire for the grapes too. And you will be lucky if you eat ten grapes.

"You lose the desire after eating two patties. It has a taste that is neither good nor bad. You eat it without expectation. You lose the desire for any other kind of food. Your stomach will shrink, you will lose weight and you will feet great. You will be agile, active and creative. You will accomplish many things that you have never known before in your life.

"Eating rice cakes is an opportunity to get rid of fat and excess weight and to trade an undesirable, bulky, clumsy carcass for a fine body. Then you could go back to being a human being again. You will feel better with your own people. Take your clothes off, stand in front of a tall mirror, look at your body and say, "Bye bye, fat. Bye bye, bulge. Bye bye, bulk. Bye bye, carcass. Hello beautiful body!"

൙൚

If you are honest with yourself, your self will be honest with you.

Desires

Desires are natural and desires are luring, but if they overwhelm you, you will be like a lost puppy infested with ten thousand ticks. They will suck your blood and your personality will be dried like parched clay in the desert.

Desires are natural, but if you let them conduct your life, you will be like a mouse in the skin of a human being.

Desires are natural, but if you go along with them, misery will go along with you.

Desires are natural, but if you don't limit them, they will limit your mind and you will have half a mind.

Desires are natural and desires are beautiful, but they create a dark veil between you and your real being.

Desires are natural and desires are sweet, but they are the product of the negative self. And the negative self is the product of darkness which will keep you on the dark side of life. And the light of heaven will never enter your heart.

Desires are natural and desires are pleasurable, but they are blocks to the beautiful eternity inside the heart.

Desires are natural and desires are boundless temptation. If your spirit is bound by them, your mind will be scattered and your intelligence will be dull and your mentality will be tarnished.

Yes And No

Say "No" to your ego desire and you will be at peace ever after. Say "Yes" to your ego desire and you will live in misery ever after. Inhibit the worst in you and enhance the best in you if you wish to be tranquil of mind and your days to be beautiful like a sailboat cruising the sea of life and the shore of time.

Say "Yes" to your lust and greed and you will be like a newspaper in a storm over the sea. If the storm stops, the sea will get the newspaper. Say "No" to your lust and greed and in every breath you will inhale peace and life around you will be filled with peace.

And how will you do that? By making your thoughts work for you instead of against you. Remember that you are given a great power by thinking and having thoughts. Don't underestimate that power. If you do, it will backfire on you. A negative thought is a polluted spring and fountain of misery and disaster.

Having negative thoughts will sap the vital force within you, exhaust you and make you weak and sick. Your face will be as gloomy as if it had been twisted by a monkey wrench and your face will look like a monkey's. If they push the monkey wrench into the computer, the message comes out loud, saying, "Oh my God, I know now why they call me Monkey Wrench."

Thought is a power that you need to understand, to appreciate, to respect and to be thankful for. Working with your thought positively will open closed doors for

The Enchanted Oasis of the Ringed Dove

you. Working with your thought negatively will close all the doors for you. Any time you abuse your thinking, it will take you to darkness. The more you abuse your thought, the more you regress in your consciousness.

When a constant thought is negative, you will be not much different from a cow. The more you abuse your thinking and thought, the more your face will look like the face of a cow. When the face completely has the look of a cow, then when you see cows, you will start to moo like the cows. You will have the notion that you are feeling homesick for the herd. You will run and join them proclaiming, "Oh boy! No, no, it is NOT a 'boy.' It is, Oh boy 'bull!' That is more like it. Here I can become like the cows and I don't have to think anymore."

But if you want the other direction, the highest and the best, don't use your thoughts to put yourself down or tear yourself down or make yourself negative. Don't permit your thoughts to become an instrument of your ego, negative self and lower desires. Be positive and turn your thoughts into a sweet spring and a fountain of progress. Let your thoughts be a stimulant for spirit and whatever is in the world will be harmonious to you.

Constant positive thought will open the spirit in you. The material in the world will be seen in the eye of the spirit. It is only when you are in the spirit that you will be able to see the spirit in material. If you are not in the spirit, you will see the form of material. And material has its moment and it loses its attraction and pleasure sooner than you think.

When there is no spirit, you seek comfort, confirmation and assurances from appearance, decoration, embellishment and so on. But the confirmation, comfort and assurances you get only confirm and assure your outer look. The inside of you is no more than hollow bamboo. And the spirit can't be found anywhere inside of you. When there is no spirit, you are only left with a form having a tarnished intelligence. Forms seek material in the form of clothes, objects, ornaments and decoration. And even a plastic toy has sway on a man without spirit. But the irony of the matter is that when a man is empty like hollow bamboo, that empty hollow bamboo can't be satisfied or content even if he is offered all the department stores, all the malls, all the shops and all that is in them. He will still not have enough.

He will shout "I want more! I don't have enough!" That tiny little hole in the bamboo becomes as big as a black hole and will swallow the world. And the man screams, "I want more!"

When there is no spirit, the lust and greed stretch themselves as far as the infinite. Such is the case of materialistic man who is a sad story in this beautiful existence. Sorrow, despair and sadness are the traits of the materialistic man in advanced, civilized societies. Separation and dispersion make him lonely. If he wears a golden ring round his neck, it will tie him to perpetual misery and make him blind to the reality.

And Hurrah to the Renaissance and the Industrial Revolution!

෴

Real change in the world becomes real when the spirit becomes real and when the light of the spirit fills the heart with love.

High Level of Knowledge

Spirit is the final evolution of humanity. When the spirit is in full command, then humanity will flourish to a high level of knowledge, wisdom and understanding where beatitude and spirit reflect each other. It is only when you go to the spirit that you will be beautiful and your mind will be tranquil and your emotions will be harmonious and creative. And your heart will contain nothing but peace.

Peace is the highest form of energy that emanates from the spirit. The spirit is a force and a power that exists in the universe, in the cosmos and in the space. If you are able to be in contact with it, you will be transformed to a unique and different human being. That force exists everywhere near you and around you. But you cannot see it, because you are in a dark existence and incapable of finding that power. It is like you are in a night that is pitch dark and you cannot see the tip of your nose. If you turn the light on, you will see the tip of your nose, your arms, legs and body. And if there is a vase with a bouquet of roses, you will be able to see the beautiful color and smell the perfume of the roses.

But in the dark, you are still able to smell the perfume of the roses. And this is an indication or a sign, regardless of how far a human being has degenerated with material technology, lust, desires, the wrong and abusive use of the senses, corruption and being tortured by the ego. In this so called advanced civilization, he carries loads and loads of affliction which bend his back and keep him constantly exhausted, nervous and tense. He seeks comfort and solace in wine, liquor and all the addictive, artificial foods and drink. Under all the horrendous conditions of darkness which take him far away from consciousness, spirit, decency, respect and honor, he loses his humanity and becomes a puppet that functions by pulling the strings.

A man will not know himself or who the other people are around him or what he is doing or what is happiness. He cannot have real communication with other people. He cannot relate to himself and they cannot relate to him. He is bored and they are bored. They think of each other as a heavy burden. And the only time that burden falls down is when he is in communion with beer, wine or liquor, hash or drugs.

Insensitive Life in a Barrel

This is truly a dark existence. It is the bottom of a barrel which has black crude oil in the bottom of it with twenty mice, ten rats and five cats, who all jumped in it because a rotten piece of meat was in the barrel. They all died and have been there for fifty days. They all had the notion of a having a great dinner and celebration.

A man in this advanced, progressive, materialistic, technical society falls into this barrel and gets stuck there indefinitely, possibly until the end of his life. He gets conditioned to living in the barrel with the stinking mice, rats and cats. He smokes and drinks and breathes dead air and smog because the barrel is located in an industrial area with many factories around it that vie with each other to produce poisonous gas and put death in the air.

The Enchanted Oasis of the Ringed Dove

This man gets so conditioned in that environment of poisonous gases and yellow and gray air that he makes a door in the barrel to go to work in the adjacent factory. He thinks he is the luckiest person in the world because he doesn't have to drive back and forth to his job.

He drinks at night from the barrel next to a little pool filled with black crude oil. And he thinks again that he is lucky to be drinking and watching the black crude oil because he knows without the black oil he would have no job and then he would be starving. Then he would be forced to eat the dead mice, rats and cats. And, he wonders, even if he was forced to eat them, how long they would last and what he would do after that? The only alternative left would be to commit suicide.

Despite this degenerated existence which comes from sheer ignorance of what the real reality is and being in pitch darkness, a man is still able to smell a faint scent of the fragrance of the spirit, just like smelling the perfume of the roses in the dark. Man is created with the spirit but his actions, ignorance and corruption bring him to the lowest of the low in the creation of God.

God said in the Koran, "God created the soul with a balance and inspired it with corruption and perfection. He who will purify his soul will find happiness and he who will corrupt it will ruin himself."

Peace is the highest form of energy that emanates from the spirit. When the spirit is not there and peace is not coming from the spirit, then peace is coming from the intellect. And the intellect has shortcomings. Then the peace becomes shortcoming peace, which is more in tune with homecoming with a lot, a lot of desires for two fried eggs, toast with marmalade, coffee with cream and sugar and afterwards a double hot, apple pie with four scoops of vanilla ice cream to commemorate the great event of homecoming.

Adnan Sarhan

Mr. Wisefish and the Grandson of Geronimo

Of course, Mr. Wisefish never missed a day in his life without apple pie. It is a must after lunch and supper. For the homecoming, having apple pie, after breakfast is a bonus because homecoming is not everyday. Actually it is just an excuse to indulge because it makes no difference to him whether it is homecoming or not homecoming. Even when he wakes up at any hour of the night, it will be most difficult for him to sleep unless he charges to the refrigerator for the pie in the freezer where he stuck boxes of ice cream.

He claims it is an old Indian recipe that was given to him by the grandson of Geronimo, to soothe his sympathetic nervous system after smoking the peace pipe with him to commemorate peace in the Four Corners. I wonder if the Indian thought of other corners besides or beyond only these Four Corners? I know that the front of the television has four corners and the back has four corners, the top has four corners, the bottom has four corners and the right side has four corners and the left side has four corners. So if you add all these four corners you will have twenty-four corners. A room has four corners and if you use the television logic, there are twenty-four corners. In a house, you come out with quite a few corners. And actually almost everything is made of corners except the space and the earth which is round and round.

I wonder if the Red Indian knew about the round and round of the earth, because the four corners they were talking about would be rounded with round and round. And they would be running on a pinto horse to catch the corner. And the corners go round and round. And possibly the merry-go-round has some mystical aspect of round and round. So leave your pinto horse and jump on the horse of the merry-go-round and go round and round. Fill your heart with joy, forget the Four Corners and sing "Around the World in Eighty Days."

Now, about the Indian recipe of hot apple pie and vanilla ice cream. It does not go really too far back in the Indian annals, but it was discovered by the grandson of Geronimo, who used to go by the name Nimonimo.

Mr. Wisefish was travelling on his way to the homecoming event to celebrate with his charming beautiful daughter, Desiree, because she had been chosen as Triple Queen of the Homecoming, the Queen of the Horticulture, the Queen of the Animal Husbandry School and the Queen, in general, of the Homecoming. But he stopped in Riodoso to rest and to have breakfast or brunch. Actually he already had had an early bird breakfast, but his habit while travelling was to have breakfast and brunch and then lunch and afternoon break. Wherever he saw a coffee shop, he had to stop and eat. Whether breakfast, lunch, dinner or in between, it's all the same, food is food. You could lose count of all the stops he made.

Ice Cream, Pie and the Nerve Pinch

He stopped at Chuck Wagon Steak Place for his breakfast and that is where he met the grandson of Geronimo. He called himself Nimonimo. This was to camouflage his real name so that no one would know who he was, because his grandfather was Geronimo, who had the last battle with the United States Cavalry on a little mountain where he fortified himself between Riodoso and Alamogordo, which is on the way to the White Sands in New Mexico.

Adnan Sarhan

Behind the Chuck Wagon was a gathering of Indians in a Pow Wow to do the Four Corner Dance. Nimonimo took Wisefish with him and Wisefish participated in the Four Corner Dance. He was so enthusiastic and exalted that he wanted to be one of the regular dancers so he could come whenever they met. After the dance, he told Nimonimo that he always had a pinch in his sympathetic nervous system that caused him to limp and kick involuntarily at any object that came near him. Nimonimo told him that he had exactly the same problem and that he discovered a way to cure it after intense research.

He told him that he used to work in 31 Flavors Ice Cream Parlor and he developed a liking and taste for all the flavors. He had a big tablespoon which he used to carry in his back pocket. When no one was around, he got his spoon and used to eat lavishly without discrimination. After a period of time, he discovered that when he ate apple pie in between the ice cream, the pinch in his back stopped. He even gave the recipe to the Grand Medicine Man, Brave Buffalo, who had the same pinch in his back and could not cure it with all his medicine.

So Nimonimo took Wisefish to 31 Flavors, but before that, he stopped at a grocery store and bought three pies: one apple for the healing and one cherry for dessert and one pecan for an appetizer. He took him to the back door of 31 Flavors and there, in a little room, he brought a tub of ice cream three-quarters full. Nimonimo dumped all the pies in it and told him, "This is the recipe of all and everything whic not only gets rid of the pinch in the back, but will make any sickness or ailment, psychic, mental or emotional disappear. Your waist will be streamlined and your face will be shining with a smile and you will be as strong as a buffalo.

They both had a contest to see which one could eat the fastest and which one could consume the most. After

The Enchanted Oasis of the Ringed Dove

the contest, Wisefish started screaming, "I feel great! I lost the pinch! I feel strong and happy!"

Nimonimo said, "I knew it would work."

Wisefish said, "Thank you, Nimonimo, you saved my back and my mind. I have to be running along to be on time for the homecoming and for my lovable Desiree who is hoping to be the Queen, not only queen, but three queens! This makes me very proud. And if my daughter is the queen, then I must be king. After you cured my back, I feel like a real King.

Desiree and the Mystery of the Veil

Just a short time before the homecoming, Desiree was getting ready to ride on a golden throne on the float in the parade. Actually, the throne was an old chair thrown in the basement that they brought up and covered with golden wrapping paper. On the top of it, they installed a crown made of plastic with a golden color.

Desiree was in a hurry and on roller skates rolling in the aisles of the dorm. She came to the mirror to put lipstick on. She thought if she put a lot of red lipstick on to make her lips really wide, then the people would really think she was a queen. So she put her lower lip between her teeth to paint the lipstick on to make it look bigger. But since she was in a hurry and was leaning on the dresser, the skate rolled away. She fell and hit her mouth on the desk and cut her lips. A commotion took place and eventually they cleaned away the blood and put a bandage on.

The problem was what was she going to do on the float? So her roommate came up with the ingenious idea that they should announce her as Queen Cleopatra. Queen Cleopatra used to be mysterious and mystical and she knew about the self. Wherever she appeared in public, she put on a veil that covered the face below the eyes. She used to put on blue mascara and also artificial eye lashes, black and long. And her eyebrows, with a deep curve, were like the bow of an archer.

The friend told her, "So you are going to have all of that and you will be Cleopatra of nowadays. From time to time, while you are on the throne, give a wink to the people. From time to time, lift up your royal scepter in a greeting gesture. The golden cobra snake around your head will make you look majestic and beautiful, as if you were the twin sister of Cleopatra."

After the parade and the celebration, Desiree told her father that she has a pinch in her back. Wisefish told her, "Come with me quickly to the car and I will take you to the best doctor and you will be cured immediately."

So he took her to 31 Flavors. He had with him an apple pie and he ordered ten scoops of vanilla. They ate it all and her pinch was gone. And they lived happily ever after.

৪৩

The spirit makes the ego run away just like a mouse running for his life from a hungry cat. If the spirit is not there, the ego becomes the cat and the man becomes the mouse. But the ego cat eats steak and hangs the mouse from his tail with a string to torture him. When you see a person negative, anxious, tense and confused, be sure that that person is a mouse hung from his tail by a string and the ego cat is playing yo-yo with him. The ego loves to play yo-yo with the person who venerates the ego.

Man and His Thought

Life without spirit is as valuable as a broken bottle of beer in a garbage dump. A man with spirit is always in the present because the creation is always in the present. The creation loves a man with spirit who is in the present. It smiles to him and keeps him in contact with the tranquil pleasure of the spirit. The essence of creation is spirit. And in the spirit, the past, present and future are all one.

When a man becomes awake, there will be between him and the reality, a mysterious hidden field of subtle energy which manifests itself in a deep, intuitive, perceptive intelligence with charm, beauty, expanded feeling, extended sensitivity, discernment and awareness. He will be taken to level after level, to witness an unknown reality of inner knowledge, *ma'arifa*, and a love that is unique, the love of the wakeful state, which is pure, clean and transcendent.

To compare this love to the ordinary love that a human being knows, is like a man having forty bottles of beer in a bar one night while trying to be courteous to his girlfriend and telling her all about love. Love of the wakeful state is a love that comes from the spirit and goes to the spirit. It seeks the spirit. It adores the spirit and lives in the spirit. And in the spirit, it thrives. Spirit is the essence of love and love is the heart of spirit. There is no spirit without love and no love without spirit, in the wakeful state, known in Arabic as *al-hadhra*.

Adnan Sarhan
The Forgetful State

The source of the wakeful state is the living spirit which is unknown to a man who is not awake and who is in a forgetful state. When a man is in a forgetful state, he is a victim of his senses. The senses control him and tear his energy, vitality and creativity to pieces. Whatever he does has a feeling of gloom. He is never, never at peace with himself and never knows what peace really is. He is tense and stiff and always thinking about how to solve all the problems of all the people in the world, but he cannot solve even his own problems. He will never solve his problems for the rest of his life, nor will he solve the problems of any other person. He is swimming against a torrential current and is unable to swim with the waves by riding the waves.

Man in the forgetful state is heedless and unaware. He thinks he is sure of what he is doing, but sorrow and unpleasantness are always his abode. His body is unbalanced. He is divested of anything that has to do with real intelligence. His limited intellect limits him to information, gadgets, tools, machines, computers, calculators, screwdrivers and so on.

He reads magazines and newspapers that talk about heat waves, cold waves, crime waves, problems, comics and other related matters. Without these publications, he is lost as though he has fallen in space from a spaceship. Without the newspapers, coffee and cigarettes, his life will be a disaster. Not that he is not in a disaster already, but the second disaster is like a security blanket that gives him warmth. The second disaster is the vain publications, the coffee and the cigarettes. And the first disaster is living in a false state.

Life without spirit is a dead life. No amount of makeup or powder-puffing or pampering the self or eating or drinking or pie or even all the cookies in the entire world will be able to revive the spirit when the spirit has sunk into a dark abyss of lust, greed, selfishness, hate, corruption, confusion, anxiety, fear, disturbance and all the negative wickedness when the ego is in command.

When the ego is in command, be sure that the ego will use you as a racquetball. It will hit you so hard that you will bounce from wall to wall. And in the space between the walls, you won't have time to think of what to do, because you are hit and kicked so hard that the hit and kick becomes a normal existence. After all, if you become a racquetball, what chance will you have to avoid the hit and kick or to protest the wall, let alone to be a human being.

Man Between Spirit and No Spirit

This is the fate of millions and millions of people in the consumer system, to consume their humanity and spirit for the sake of a plastic duck and to sacrifice their peace, tranquility and honor on the altar of the ego with its congregation of wickedness, corruption, phoniness and ignorance.

> *A man with spirit is a beautiful creature.*
> *A man without spirit is an ugly creature.*
> *A man with spirit is positive by nature.*
> *A man without spirit is negative by nature.*
> *A man with spirit has a charming disposition.*
> *A man without spirit has a gloomy disposition.*
> *A man with spirit knows love.*
> *A man without spirit does not know love.*
> *A man with spirit knows the love of spirit.*

A man without spirit knows the love of greed and selfishness.

A man with spirit has a living heart and his love is alive.

A man without spirit has a dead heart and his love is dead.

A man with spirit is a human being and his heart contains the universe.

A man without spirit has cold icy eyes and human passion is dead in them.

A man with spirit is the friend of God.

A man without spirit is the friend of the devil.

A man with spirit is the master of himself.

A man without spirit is the slave of himself.

A man with spirit, the world dances in his eyes.

A man without spirit, the world is gloomy in his eyes.

A man with spirit, harmony resides in his mind and heart.

A man without spirit, disturbance resides in his mind and heart.

A man with spirit is a vessel of spirit and the time is the sea and the days are smooth waves that induce pleasure and tranquility.

A man without spirit is the vessel of the devil and the time is a stormy dark sea and the days are sharp thorny rocks of painful problems and disaster.

A man with spirit has a contented heart.

A man without spirit has a tormented heart.

A man with spirit, his love is adorned with joy, pleasure and contentment which make love alive and life alive with the love of the moment.

A man without spirit, his love is marred with selfishness, lust and lifeless love.

A man with spirit is blessed by God.

A man without spirit is blessed by the devil.

The Enchanted Oasis of the Ringed Dove

A man with spirit does not think with the intellect, because the intelligence of the heart bypasses the intellect in the head which works on assumptions and requires a lot of thinking and confusion and makes him tired and weak. But, the heart intelligence is not only direct and to the point, it also gives you energy, vitality and strength.

The spirit connects you to reality and this is what makes you real. The spirit within you flows out of you and into the depth of reality, while the spirit of reality flows into your heart. Your spirit plunges in a universal, cosmic sea of wave after wave of pure intelligence and affirmation of love which fills all the universal space to the infinite. And your heart basks in that sea of love, fills up and gets drunk with love, peace and tranquility.

There is no division between the spirit and the world. The world is a beautiful extension of the spirit when the spirit is alive. When the spirit is dead, the world is dead and life is lifeless. People are not connected with reality or themselves. When the spirit is alive, the world becomes a garden of roses and people become drunk with its nectar.

Man Under Material

Material is created to serve people. People are not created to serve material. A man should be the master and material the slave. But if the material becomes the master and the man is the slave, the man is doomed to destruction and ruin.

When man becomes a slave to the material, the material lures him, controls him and saps his energy by making him weak and dependent on the material to bring comfort to him. Because he is weak, tense and nervous, with scores of ailments and problems, the material will withdraw its comfort from him by the command of the balance of events of the invisible world. The man will become the victim of a false reality of hope and expectation. The false reality becomes his only known reality. He becomes a false man in a false reality.

He is imperfect and incomplete, just an image of a man, not in the image of God but in the image of a corrupted man. He thinks he is pure and an important member of society when really he is corrupted. He will corrupt the environment and the nature around him, thinking that he is creating beauty and showing progress. Because sensitivity and discernment have been gone for a long time, if he really ever had sensitivity and discernment, the man becomes corrupted and evil in the materialistic system.

Material without spirit imposes a rigid disastrous way of life and brings another death to the man besides the natural death. This imposed death is known as the greater death. The natural death is the lesser death. In the greater death, the man is living, but the spirit in him is dead. He is like a machine. He walks, talks and functions without the intelligence of the heart. He laughs, but his laughter screeches like the noise of a dying machine. He is a burden on himself and society, while society is a burden on itself and on him. In this dark existence and reality, the mood is full of tension, confusion, fear, anxiety and disturbance.

Man With a Dead Heart

When you have a whole society with the attributes of the greater death, you have a society of the macabre. Cab drivers will have the attributes of Frankenstein, the

The Enchanted Oasis of the Ringed Dove

Wolfman and Dracula. And Vincent Price will be their director with Boris Karloff as his assistant and dispatcher.

Their night is not night and their day is not day. Their night is filled with horror and their day is filled with disappointment. They cannot differentiate between day and night. Their senses are dead, their vision is dead, their awareness is dead, their understanding is dead, their perception is dead, their feeling is dead, their emotion is dead, their sight is dead, their taste is dead, their touch is dead.

Because all of these things are dead within them, the people want to have some form of order to give themselves some kind of balance and security against the odd tribulation. So they create all kinds of ordinances, rules, orders and laws that are fit only for a man with a dead heart. A man with dead heart is not sensitive. He is clumsy, unaware, without manners, conduct, behavior, respect, dignity, honor or personality. His disposition is a mixture of King Kong and Godzilla.

God said in the Koran, "We have made every man's action to cling to his neck." And God also said, "Whoever is blind in this world will be blind in the hereafter."

When the spirit is dead in a man, the ego replaces the spirit. When the spirit is gone, the man is gone. This means his essence and beauty are gone. What is left is crudity, ugliness and heaviness, not a physical heaviness, but heaviness in his presence. If he comes nears you, he will give you the feeling as if the roof of the room has fallen down on you and you cannot breathe. So this is heavy presence which is the opposite of light presence.

When people are in this miserable state, the ego becomes the greatest thing in their life. Ego is the biggest obstacle to truth, reality and happiness. Ego is a blinding force that sees the dark as light. Ego is a sheer work of evil. It obliterates the senses, the intellect, the intelligence and the spirit. Ego is the ideal idol of lust, greed, selfishness, avarice, ignobility, ignominy, pride, ignorance, corruption and stupidity. It is better to be nonexistent than to exist with these fabulous credentials. But these fabulous credentials find a fertile soil in materialistic societies which don't know anything about spirit and consciousness.

Firmly and unshakably the people believe that ego and pride are the cause of success, happiness and getting ahead in the world. They think they are very, very civilized and on the highest pinnacle of progress, which gives them cars, televisions, typewriters, computers, wallpaper, noisemakers and colorful balloons to blow up on New Year's Eve, to create an appropriate sound for welcoming the New Year. And two eggs sunny-side-up, buttered toast with marmalade, coffee with cream and sugar makes a good breakfast for the first morning of the New Year. Or, if you wish, steak and eggs.

When the Ego Wears a Thousand Shoes

A person in this advanced civilized society could have fifty belts or maybe hundreds to match his trousers and forty or fifty or more pairs of shoes. This is a normal number. So when Imelda Marcos, the first lady of the Philippines, looked up to these advanced, civilized materialists, her ego told her that she too could be an advanced, civilized materialist. She looked at these civilized materialistic people as ideal idols of progress and sophistication. It is no wonder that she imitated them and acquired a thousand pairs of shoes! Because she was ignorant of spirit, she imitated ignorant people, then she became doubly ignorant.

The Enchanted Oasis of the Ringed Dove

To imitate lustful, materialistic and spiritually ignorant people will do no justice to your humanity and will be a base deed. A civilization without consciousness or spirit breeds corruption and the state of life becomes unstately, crude, base and meaningless.

The ego makes people stupid. Stupid people have stupid personalities which are very apparent in their faces. It is like the personality you see on the face of a donkey. But the face of a donkey shows innocence and he is indifferent to any situation. He doesn't know the word ego nor its meaning or its existence.

The ego makes people stupid, destroying their intelligence and abolishing it completely. The word 'stupid' makes all the difference in the world. If you are not stupid, you will be on the top of the world. If you are stupid you will be in the underworld.

৸৹৻ৎ

The stronger the spirit, the more you are alive, vivacious and a real human being. When you have no spirit you will have a lot in common with a coat, car, radio or shoes. When you wear the shoes, they walk. If you take them off, they stop. The thinking of a man without spirit is like the shoes, merely for accommodation. In materialistic societies, intelligence of the heart does not exist.

The Cow

The importance of a man without spirit is like the importance of a kite in the hand of a child. Spirit is the door to the secret beauty of reality. A man without spirit is a reject creature of the universe. When you find the essence of reality, peace will be all around you.

Without spirit, you cannot escape tension, confusion, misery, anxiety, doubt and one thousand problems a day. There is no peace and no rest even with the best of education and the most in wealth and the highest in social life, because something is missing. What is missing is the best in life, the spirit. If you have it, you can have all the other things in life. If you don't have it, you can have all the other things in life, but no spirit. And that is back to where you started.

Without spirit, all that you have is trash. With the spirit, all that you have will be like precious stones. The spirit puts spirit in the objects around a man who has the spirit. Spirit attracts spirit.

Any man who puts an effort toward the spirit will get the spirit. For this effort, you need discipline. For the discipline, you need action. For the action, you need will power. For the will power, you need positive thought. For the positive thought, you need right intention. For the right intention, you need faith. For the faith, you need to be a human being.

The Enchanted Oasis of the Ringed Dove

A human being has all the beautiful traits and excellent faculties that are special to him alone and not available to the rest of the creatures. A kangaroo, a rabbit and a duck, for instance, do not have any of these qualities. A cow can not comprehend the miraculous things a man has. Because the cow does not have intelligence, she is not interested in any of these qualities. She thinks all of that is a mishmash mashed potato and the best thing in life is grass.

She has a short cut way to the grass which she calls "direct to the grass." She learned it from a man when he said "direct from the factory." So she learned something of value. But instead of saying direct from the factory, she says "direct to the grass." This is the core of the matter. This is the bottom line. This is the gist of the meadow. This is the essential of existence. This is the bare bone of all the steaks. For what is there in the world for a cow to eat except grass and grass and more grass? People eat steaks and dogs eat bones.

How Cowawi Outwitted the Rancher

"I am Cow Cowawi and I am going to tell you a secret, but you must promise not to tell this secret to anyone at all. The bottom line of the secret is that I am very happy to be a cow without intelligence. Because, if God had created me as a human being with intelligence, I am afraid I would be abusing my intelligence like many human beings who destroy their intelligence by eating steaks filled with hormones, chemicals and all kinds of injections that made them fat.

The rancher who takes care of me is very materialistic, greedy and a penny pincher, as most people who look to material and money as their savior, are. They glorify the dollar on the pretext that "In God We Trust" is written on it. So this greedy, miserly rancher of mine fills me with hormones to make me big and fat, to make more money on me, even though he knows that when people eat me they will get sick and eventually they will die. He doesn't care as long as he gets the dollar. On it is written "In God We Trust." And if God is on the dollar, to catch this nearer God is better than to catch the far way God.

"I am Cow Cowawi and I would like to advise those people who are greedy, selfish, doubtful, egotistical, negative, confused and abusive to their intelligence — the cigarette smokers, wine gulpers and junk food eaters — my advice to them is 'Clean up your act or your brain will be cut.'

"Look at me. I am Cow Cowawi. I don't do any of the things that you do, even though God didn't give me intelligence like you. I eat only grass and I am happy. You do all the things that you do and you look like scum, feel like scum and think like scum. If you want to change from this scum muddle you are in, my remedy is not to do anything the negative self wants you to do and you will be pure like a fragrant rose.

"So man, don't think of this as a cow saying. It is true that I am a cow and you are a man and man is higher than a cow. But, if a man does not use his intelligence to advance his purpose in life, his thinking will be like a cow's. I am saying it from experience and I have qualifications for that. I will explain this to you. It goes like this.

"God gave intelligence to a man.

"God did not give intelligence to the cow.

"So a cow has no idea about what intelligence can do. But I am Cow Cowawi, a little different from other cows. How I became different was a surprise to me. While I was in the field eating grass as usual, all of the sudden I became bored and I said to myself, "Eating, eating, eating. Sleeping, sleeping, sleeping. What kind of life is that? Is there any other thing that could exist in the life of a cow?"

The Miraculous Revelation of the Cow

"So I sat in meditation and Lo and Behold! Ya Hallelujah, Ya Holy Cow! Ya Secret Cow! Ya Cowabunga! Ya Cow of the Year! Ya Cow of Who's Who! Ya CoverCow of the Star Magazine! Ya Beauty Queen Cow of the Universe! Ya Holy Cow Cowawi! Ya roping cow in Texas rodeo! Ya Wooly Bully Well Woolly! Ya arrow in the bull's eye! Ya water buffalo in the swamp!

"Ya John Wayne and the trail of the lost cows! Ya Cow Cowawi hoofprint on the sidewalk in front of the Chinese theater! Ya cowboys who extol the glory of the wilderness looking after the baby cows! Ya cows who have affinity to dirty cowboys! Ya cowboys who jump on the back of the wild bull singing the praises of the firmness and the flexibility of the muscles in their thighs! Ya cows who are the millstone in all the episodes! Ya cow thieves and rustlers! Ya cows in the forefront of the Wild West papers!

"Ya cow in the wax museum on Hollywood Boulevard! Ya steak lovers wherever you are! Ya hot dog eaters with mustard and radish! Ya Arbie's roast beef! Ya Burger King! Give the queen half of your hamburger. Ya three-hour-waiting line in below-zero for McDonald hamburger in Moscow! Ya sirloin tip with gravy in a diner! Ya rib eye steak on a charcoal fire at the side of a pool!

Adnan Sarhan

"Ya Cow Cowawi bust in Hall of Fame! Ya Cowawi life-size color photo in a plush airport waiting room! Ya sheep, goats, pigs and rabbits! Ya wolf and coyotes! Ya Cowawi water-skiing in Cypress Gardens! Ya Cow Cowawi on the shoulder of Mr. Shanouk while he is doing the skiing! Ya Shanouk jumping twenty feet in the air over an obstacle! Ya Cowawi smiling with arms in the air holding a pink sign in the shape of a heart and written on it, "I Love You All," and the other arm around the neck of Mr. Shanouk! Ya spectators and tourists, laughing and applauding Cow Cowawi and Mr. Shanouk!

"What a discovery! What an ice breaking! What a grand opening! What a marvelous pioneering! Ya Wild, Wild West! Ya Cowboys! I am Cow Cowawi and I am announcing the biggest event in the world which took place in the field of grass to the field of knowledge. This is how it happened, step by step, to higher consciousness.

"While I was sitting cross-legged and cross arms concentrating on my mind, whatever little mind was there, and I was striving for a higher mind and maybe a little piece of intelligence to go along with it. Again and for the second time, Lo and Behold! The secret that protects itself revealed itself. A stream and ray of light came from heaven and hit me right on the forehead between the eyes. Instantly and without further notice, I became wise. I could read what was in the mind of a man. And I read the thoughts in the mind of my rancher.

"For weeks he has been thinking that if he makes me twice as fat, he will get twice as much money when he sells me. Immediately, I knew this man was stupid. He wasted weeks thinking about something which was bound to happen without thought.

"I started to do fasting. I didn't want to see myself as a fat cow anymore. It is repulsive and degrading and not becoming for someone like me who has discovered new knowledge. Ignorant cows get fat. I am not ignorant anymore. I am wise and I am going to be like a gazelle. Gazelles are beautiful and God is beautiful and He loves beauty. He opens the gate of heaven for the gazelles to come and entertain the prophets.

"There is no going back to what I was before, a brainless cow. It is not possible, because when the rays of light hit me, I started to hear clear words vibrating in my head and body and for seven days they said, "If God wishes something, He will say, 'Be,' and it will be." This is written in the Koran.

Cowawi's Philosophical Advice to Man

"So man, let me tell you about something you have, but you have abused. You have under your command the greatest gift in the universe, the existence and the creation. You have the intelligence of the heart — dynamic, creative, powerful, miraculous, the source of life, love, peace, beauty, magic, joy, contentment, satisfaction, generosity, abundance, tranquility, purity, spirit and a smile from the everlasting fountain of *baraka* (blessing), consciousness, awareness, feeling, evolution, respect and honor.

"God said in the Koran, 'If you count the blessings of God you will find no number to contain them.'

"And you, man, when you start to count the pennies and calculate what you have, will lose the blessings of God.

"You have replaced the intelligence of the heart, which is part of God's intelligence, the living force, the source of knowledge, the inner knowledge and the vital living energy, without which, the universe will not function. The sun will be no sun and the moon will be no moon and the stars will be no stars."

But God takes care of the universe. God said in the Koran, "By the sun and his glorious splendor, by the moon as she follows him, by the day as it shows up the sun's glory, by the night as it conceals it, by the firmament and its wonderful structure, by the earth and its wide expanse."

"It is the cosmos which is behind that magical creation that you are a part of. But when man obliterates the intelligence of the heart and substitutes it with the intellect of the head and listens to his emotions, senses, desires, whims and the negative self and operates from his ego instead of love and peace, he falls in a state of forgetfulness, chaos, confusion, struggle and problems. The man has tricked himself out of the real and into the unreal.

Mohammed said, "It is your own doing that puts you in paradise or hell and you think it is destiny. But you make your own destiny."

Cow Cowawi said, "Hey man, let me tell you something. You know the natural way for a cow is to eat and eat and eat and to be fat and fat and fat. But I have discovered that when you do something spiritual and develop in the spirit, you lose weight. Cows, who don't have brains, have no way to know when to stop eating. It is only when the cow has no mind that she will eat forever. Food is the only activity that exists in the life of mindless cows. I thank God that I do not belong to that category anymore. So if you are fat and you want to change, my remedy is to be in love with the spirit. The spirit will feed you cosmic energy which will cut a big percentage of the food out of your menu."

The Enchanted Oasis of the Ringed Dove
Consciousness and Shallow Thought

Cow Cowawi said, "When the intelligence of the heart opens, you will be free from thought. Intelligence of the heart means you are in the realm of the spirit. In spirit there is no thinking. In the spirit, things just happen. When you think and are not in the spirit, it means you want to arrive at something that you do not know. When you are not there, you try through the thought to get there. But when you are in the spirit, you are there. It is exactly like when you memorize poetry and you spend a lot of time doing it. When it is memorized and you become in command, you do not need to memorize it anymore because it is already memorized.

"So it is the same with spirit, when you get it, you are there. The spirit is a knowledge that operates through complete and perfect inspiration. There is no room in this place for a thought.

"If you want to know if this is really so, the best way to know is to get the spirit first. Then you will have first hand knowledge. Then you will know what no one knows when they are not in the spirit. When you are not in the spirit, you never know and all your life you will try to know but you still won't know as long as you don't know the spirit.

"But when you are in the spirit, you will be finished with all the muzzled knowledge which is the shallow knowledge, or the worldly knowledge, or the scholastic knowledge. This is the knowledge of diversion which leads to tension, confusion and anxiety. When you free yourself from this muzzle, you will no longer be deceived. And you will say, 'Thank God, for getting me out of that fraudulent world.'

"So when you find the hidden knowledge, put all your shallow thoughts which are not connected with spirit, consciousness or humanity, in a plastic trash bag and offer it to people who love thought, as a Christmas gift. Wrap the bag in red and green ribbons and write on the card which is attached to it, "With my best love, I offer you my best thought. Good luck. Enjoy it and have a panel discussion. And may the goddess, Muse, amuse you. She is the goddess of pleasure, poetry, music, dance, art and delight. Her companion is Apollo who is the best musician and the best thinker and he will conduct you through the night."

"You should know that shallow, intellectual thoughts are the biggest obstacle for the worldly people. These thoughts keep them in the world and keep them at bay from knowing reality. It keeps them in sheer ignorance from knowing who they are and they will never know peace except as a word or a thought, no more and no less.

The Koran said, "There are those whose efforts are wasted in the life of the world and they deem that they are doing well in performance."

"So if you want to know, just put the idea that you want to know in your head and strive to go deep in yourself, then you will find what you want to know."

The Present is Heaven on Earth

Cow Cowawi said, "Time has value, importance and beauty. You only thrive in the time that is in your hand. The only time that you can hold on to is the time that is in your hand. For how can you hold on to something that is not in your hand? It is the now. It is the present. It is the moment that is in your hand."

The time in your hand says to you, "I am here. I am with you. I am your contentment. I am your pleasure and

The Enchanted Oasis of the Ringed Dove

joy giver. I am the life, the love. I make you tranquil and pleasant. I give you peace which is the gift of eternity. I soothe your mind. I put rhythm in your heart and your heart beats to the moment. And the moment dances to your heart and your heart dances with the moment and life becomes a dance. Life is a dance when you are living it.

"You are only living when you are graced and blessed in the moment, by the moment. The moment is the fountain of serenity. The moment says, "I am a messenger to you, a messenger of eternity. I bring you a message of eternal joy. I am joy and tranquility. I am peace and delight. I am faith and trust. I am truth and reality. I am in the moment because I am the moment. I am honor, respect and dignity. I am simple, tolerant and generous.

"I am the time and the time is me. I am the profound depth of intelligence and intelligence is me. I am the beautiful spring of essence and essence is me. I am the perfume of life and the fragrance of a smile. I am the living spark and spirit that shines in the eyes. I am the sweet taste of heaven and I am heaven in your heart. I am charm, beauty, delight, happiness, tranquility, serenity and the pleasure of life and the joy of love, peace contentment, harmony, existence, intelligence and truth. And I am in the present all the time. With you, I am the moment that never fades, that never goes away.

"I am the boundary of the present. If you transgress this boundary by going to the future, which is unknown, and this the boundary of God, then you will become lost in the future and you will become unknown to yourself. And while you are living in the present, the present will disclaim you and the present is lost from your hands, like a pearl slipping from your hands to the sea. You will swim all your life to find it, but it is gone.

For the pearl, you will suffer in this life in a sea of transient temptations of weak, wicked desires and corruption, thinking happiness only comes from the pleasures of the senses, material and technology which bring you the most in comfort. But, as long as there is no spirit in this comfort, you will toil and sweat with apprehension, anxiety and unrest. You become a prisoner of your comfort and none of this incomplete, imperfect technology, which is built on lust, greed, selfishness and corruption, does you any good. It makes you the most stupid creature on the face of the earth. A snail's life is more perfect and complete comfort than yours. If the snail does not live in comfort, he will die.

"If a man is not in comfort with spirit, he is like a dead fish that died of pollution from the excessive trash thrown in the sea. No amount of liquor or drugs will bring life to him. No cocktail parties or orgies will revive him. No amount of food or drink will do him any good, but will make him a fat slob, clumsy, lazy, weak, wicked, ignorant and a first class zombie of the universe."

Miss Universe, the Pleasure of the Heart

"Hallelujah to the Beauty Queen of the Universe and the brainless zombies who seek the spirit from a spiritless queen. What an evening of delight and pleasure to see Miss Universe smiling and holding her lips to her ears with a string to keep her permanent smile. Those zombies wonder what kind of toothpaste she uses so they can go to the drugstore and get that particular brand, so that they can have lovely white teeth to cover their yellow stained teeth from all the coffee, cigarettes and the chocolate mousse cake.

The Enchanted Oasis of the Ringed Dove

"Then in the contest for the coming year, they will be able to smile back to Miss Universe. They will be stretching their lips to show their white teeth which vie with the queen's. And who knows? They might stand a chance to be Mr. Universe, only they do not know about the invisible string which holds Miss Universe's lips to her ears in a permanent smile.

"Those ignorant people! If only they knew that real beauty is in the spirit and not in the spiritless, plastic face of Miss Universe! If they had the spirit, all women would be Beauty Queens of the Universe and all men would be Beauty Kings of the Universe. Then they would have all the comfort and whatever they did will be perfect. Their manner, behavior and conduct would be excellent. Their minds would be clean and love would be in their hearts. They would be excellent human beings and have the smile of spirit. God would give them respect, dignity, personality, beauty and presence. All the misery, confusion, disturbance, sickness, weakness, complication, selfishness, greed and ego would disappear.

Baby Ruth

Ego is the biggest contributing factor to the misery of people who have no spirit. They cling to their ego as a child clings to the hem of his mother, crying and screaming for candy.

"Mommy, Mommy, I must have a Baby Ruth or I will die. You have a baby and I am your baby and I must have a Baby Ruth. Nothing else will do. Baby Ruth is the only one. And I will scream to the end of the world for a Baby Ruth. Baby Ruth is in my brain and Baby Ruth is in my heart and Baby Ruth is in my being. I love Baby Ruth. I will scream all night and you will not be able to sleep. So you must give me a Baby Ruth now! And I mean it! You must listen to me, I love Baby Ruth. All night I dream about Baby Ruth.

"Don't take this matter so lightly! It is a very serious matter. I am not like any other child. I have spirit. This is why I am talking like this. My name is Dennis. And you better do some evaluating before you think this case is closed. Baby Ruth does not recognize any cases. The only case she recognizes is in my mouth. We have good vibrations toward each other. So get me a Baby Ruth. This is final. I will stop talking now to start screaming."

When people live in the past, they have a passover personality which is a flat personality, as if a steam roller has passed over them and they come out like a flat, one dimensional sugar cookie. They fall in love with each other because everyone thinks that everyone is a sugar cookie. Love with sugar tastes better than sourdough. And they will be wrapped up in each other as if nothing else existed in life.

In Arabic there is a proverb that says, "If your sweetheart is honey, don't lick it all." This means there are other interests and matters in life to be involved in besides the sugar cookie.

When you pass by these people with flat personalities and flat sugar cookies, you will vaguely notice them as ghosts, that is, if you have the spirit. If you don't have the spirit, then you won't notice them and they won't notice you. You could say in that situation, "Mind your own business."

If they live in the future, they will lose their features. They will be puzzled and muddled. Anxiety, little by little, will destroy their intelligence. They will have no peace of mind and their value will be reduced to a lower value than the material they've won, just like the tag that says "Everything At Reduced Price" at Pic'N'Pay. But the material they've won will be trash. And because their value has been reduced below the value of the material they own, their future will be reduced to trash below the material trash.

Cow Cowawi said, "What an amazing existence this is. Here I am, a cow and God created me with a little brain. Because of my little brain, I keep eating and eating until I become fat, as is expected of me as a cow. I am a cow and what is expected from a cow but to be as fat as a cow. When you are a cow, you are a cow.

The Gifts of God and Man

"But I am Cowawi the cow and with the little brain that I have, I have to use it to advance my cause and purpose in life. As they say, 'There are as many ways to God as there are human beings.' But I am a cow and I found my way to God. Other cows, I don't know if they have ways to God. I know that they have ways to grass. But I, Cowawi, found a way to God! I have proved that my way is better than what they say, 'There are as many ways to God as there are people.' And I know for sure, since my enlightenment, that there are many ways to sink in the mud as there are people, except the very few who are able to spring up out of the mud.

"What is really baffling to me is that God gave the most excellent intelligence to men, the natural intelligence of the heart and spirit. He gave them perceptions, discernment, awareness, understanding, intuition, sensitivity, respect, justice, love and spirit. Men, one by one, dropped these fabulous gifts and treasures and lost their spirit. They started to look for the spirit in bars and bottles and found phony happiness in food, drinks and making toys to play with like a child.

Adnan Sarhan

"The great quality of men, to be in the image of God, disappeared. Instead of the image of God, they acquired a ragtag quality and a hazy dazy mentality and buried themselves in filthy factories, useless offices and shops, which are the source of anxiety and boredom. And these become the sole meaning of their existence. They became conceited and self conceit leads to destruction."

Ghazzali said, "A soul which allows its lower faculties to dominate the higher is as one who would hand over an angel to the power of a vicious beast."

"I am Cow Cowawi who is known as *behimeh*, which means 'given no intelligence' in the Arabic language. But through discipline and striving, I became enlightened. I fasted, meditated and contemplated and God took a fancy to me. He graced me with something higher than grass. I was blessed and life assumed a different perspective and vision. With the depth of intelligence and higher consciousness, reality after reality started to manifest in my heart and to my eyes. God made me thin like a gazelle and then he changed me into a beautiful gazelle with deep, dark, beautiful eyes like a deep well in the middle of a hot, scorching desert.

A Sea of Nectar and Roses

Be alive and grasp the vital force of life within you. Be alive like the sun during the day and tranquil like the moon at night. Make your thoughts positive and pure and make them come from an intention of goodness that bathes in the beautiful essence of creation. The spirit becomes a rose and you will be tender like a rose. The space between you and heaven becomes a sea that flows with the nectar of roses which rides on its waves when the waves are playing with each other and dancing with the wind, singing with the breeze, sending sparkling spray in the light of the sun, bursting with joy and falling back into the lap of the sea.

The sand says, "Beautiful waves and joyous spray, come to me. I love to be with you. Oh Sea, send your waves to dab my cheeks! My heart will rejoice in your coolness, because I am getting a little warm from the sun. You are the only one I know that keeps me cool and makes my heart jump when your waves splatter me all of a sudden with surprise. And I love it! What is better than to be by the sea, side by side?"

The space between you and heaven becomes a sea that flows with the nectar of roses. You will sail in a boat made of the leaves of roses. The sail dances in the light of the sun, with the gusts playing hide and seek with the mist. You will have a flight on the breeze to the moon and stars, to heaven, to the truth and to the beautiful reality. Your existence will be pure like honey and vibrant like the dawn in a clean sky and calm like the moon when the moon is full. You will smile with excitement when the cool breeze blows relentlessly, caressing your face in a pleasant summer night.

The trees' leaves quiver and glitter in the tantalizing silver light of the moon, tenderly overjoyed, dancing delightfully with the stars at night, drunk with the breeze. And you become drunk with them in a night of serenity, with excitement and pleasure. The heaven is your host introducing you to the night, the stars, the moon, the light and the playful dancing breeze. A smile in your heart reflects the contentment of spirit in your face. In your eyes shows the love of spirit in the light of the moon, with zest, delight and presence, in the moment that knows no bounds and no limit, when the heart becomes in oneness with the creation.

Your heart is filled with the spirit when you drink the breeze in a goblet made of the light of the moon and adorned with the stars as precious gems. You will be lifted above the material that is abusive to man and spirit and which leads a man by his nose, by his ego, greed and lust which come from darkness and drown him in the abyss of oblivion and a wasteful existence.

༄༅

Focus and concentration are the secret of the moment. The moment is the guide to the tranquil time and the time is heaven when tranquility binds you and the time together.

The Crow Who Forgot His Wings

Blind diversion and corruption become inherent characteristics of people who lust for material. All lust propagates weakness, stupidity, anxiety and tension. Lust divests human beings of their humanity. They look like human beings, but they are without feeling, sensitivity, love or imagination. They cannot relate to each other except when they have wine, liquor or drugs and coffee, sugar and sweets. It changes their human countenance to a shrivelled dead countenance.

They have the face of a dead cat who died drowning in a trashy swamp mixed with oil. The cat was pulled out of the swamp after six months and his face showed the horror of suffocation. Materialistic people are drowned in a similar swamp, but it is made of material junk that is so unreal that anyone with a little intelligence and common sense would see it as the most stupid situation a human being could sink to and plunge in, with no hope of lifting the head above that swamp to breathe the air or to see the beauty of heaven. Those people, with their shrivelled, dead countenance, have been in it so long that they don't know any other way. To them it is natural and beautiful. They will never know a real, sweet, tender, spontaneous smile which radiates the beauty and the light of the heart when the heart is filled with the blessings of heaven.

Adnan Sarhan

If a crow were to look into these faces with dead smiles, he would get so confused that he would run away, terrified, on the ground. From the shock, he would forget he had two swift wings. But while getting away, his senses would come back to him and he would say, "Oh my God, I have wings and I better fly!" And he would go to the nightingale screaming and shouting, "Help, help, help! I saw the devil!"

People with dead smiles are strangers to each other. They can't figure out what other people are like. They are not only strangers to each other, they are strangers to themselves. They never know the meaning of life or how tranquil and peaceful life is, how beautiful and inspiring, and how true life and nature are bound to each other and feel each other and enjoy each other.

Veils of darkness separate these people from the world, nature, consciousness and spirit. They never experience the present or know what is present. Because they are never in the present, it is not possible to know peace, tranquility, contentment or generosity.

Liquor, wine, drugs and the like are their diversions and consolation to get through life. Life is a burden. So to lighten that burden, they have to be drunk or drugged. What a wasteful way of life these people of material go through! Ignorance and the darkness of reality and the truth and the purpose of life, man and creation, overwhelm them day and night. The days of their life slip away without their noticing it, like dry sand slipping through the fingers of the hand when the temperature is above one hundred degrees in the Arabian desert. At the end of life, their mentality shrinks, deteriorates, crumbles and becomes equivalent to the mentality of roaches and beetles. Only, the roaches and beetles respect life and honor their existence and are thankful to God.

The Best with Good Intention

Seek the best with good intention and the hidden force of existence will take you to the best of destinations. The hidden force of existence seeks the best in existence wherever the best is manifested. Seek the best with bad intention and that hidden force will pour on you a permanent shower of anxiety, tension, fear and a miserable, unhappy existence.

Seek excellence and you will be excellent and heaven will come to you and with your eyes you will see heaven on earth. Seek less then excellence and you will be a creature without direction, like a piece of wood floating in an ocean bombarded by waves. Life there is like a sea and the waves of that sea will slap your face, mind, heart and body. You will be like a porcupine in a state of permanent shock.

So find a basement, sit in it, get rid of your shock and meditate on the leftover broken furniture. Have affinity for the furniture and imagine yourself as broken furniture. And broken furniture gravitates toward broken furniture. You are part of that situation.

Start fixing the broken furniture and say, "I will make them excellent. And if I make them excellent, I must be excellent." Keep repeating this and while the furniture becomes excellent, you will be excellent.

Be friends with your positive self. Find your negative self, catch it by the throat, squeeze it, strangle it, throw the broken furniture on it and say, "This is what you deserve!" If you don't do this, the negative self will cut you at your throat.

Know that the negative self controls ordinary people with material temptations. But, for people who follow the inner leaning, the negative self uses spiritual temptations. Spiritual temptation is when the negative self is defeated by the person and the negative self accepts the defeat and joins the person to bolster his effort, but then the negative self starts to instigate and woo the person for his accomplishments, saying he should be proud and that he is invincible to weakness. This is how the negative self tempts the person through spiritual temptation, like a thief who slips cautiously through the door of the kitchen.

If you subdue the negative self, then you are open to the inner knowledge, *ma'arifa*. The first stage of *ma'arifa* is knowledge of the self. The second stage is knowledge of the spirit. And the third stage is knowledge of God. If you seek excellence and become excellent, the cosmic power will enhance you with vitality, strength and intelligence. If you don't seek excellence you will never be excellent and you will be no more than *gihif*, a fragment of broken pottery. Arrogance, pride, conceit and vain glory are the characteristics of a weak, base and twisted mentality with dead spirit, personality and presence.

༄༅

Friends with spirit are friends for life. Friends without spirit are friends for the duration of a cup of wine in a bar.

Anger, the Man and the Donkey

If you get angry, you will become like a donkey. But a donkey does not get angry, therefore you are lower than the donkey. God will bless the donkey and give him more dignity and honor, while God will strip his blessing from you and you will have no dignity nor honor. God respects the donkey but will not respect an angry man. To be in the company of a donkey is more pleasant than to be in the company of an angry man.

Angry people have a disturbed mentality with no intelligence. Angry people are like filthy scum. If you get near them, you will be filthy scum, too. Stay away from them or your mind will be disturbed.

Angry people bark like a dog. But God created the dog to bark while He created the human being to sing and serenade in thanks to the bounty of creation, the splendid work of God. If a human being barks like a dog, then he is a dog in the form of a human being. So stay away from angry dogs or you will be barked at and get bitten.

The dog has the right to be angry. If a man is angry, he will possess all the rights of a dog, which means the man is stupid.

Bitterness, despair, disillusion and horror fill the life of angry men. The torturing flame of hellfire scorches their hearts even when they are asleep.

Adnan Sarhan

Ignorant people are controlled by their animal souls and they use all their strength and power to utterly please and indulge their desires, selfishness and stupidity.

If a donkey or a cow eating grass lifts her head up for a minute, her animal soul will scream in a terrifying voice, "Put your head down! Eat grass! I don't understand your fooling around. I am starved. I am hungry. I must have grass or I will die."

If a person is not thankful to someone who did something good for him, then he should know that he is an animal and being an animal is his perfect punishment.

Anger is a manifestation of a sick spirit. When a man is born, he is born with two forces or powers. These two forces pull away from each other. One of them is the spirit from heaven and the other is the animal soul from earth. The spirit wants to pull the man upward, while the animal soul pulls the man downward.

When an animal is born, he is born with an animal soul and only limited intelligence to deal with life. He never looks forward. He is only in the forwardness of the present.

Have you ever watched a donkey running happily in a meadow, then sitting down on a heap of grass like a king reviewing his kingdom? The donkey has never known the word "work," because he is in the present or the moment. Whatever happens, he is indifferent to it. Like carrying someone or some goods on his back, it is only a form of play. He has no concern for whatever is on his back even if it is gold. He has no attachment to it so he is free from attachment. If he became attached to what he was carrying on his back, whether it were gold or apples, and if he couldn't get it, then he would be angry and disturbed. Then, he would need to go to a psychologist.

The Enchanted Oasis of the Ringed Dove

So, the life of a donkey who is free and unattached, even to gold or apples, is better than the life of a man who is not free and whose attachments come from greed and selfishness which cause a decline in his intelligence.

Mohammed said, "Power resides not in being able to strike another, but in being able to keep the self under control when anger arises."

Mohammed also said, "Happy is the person who finds fault with himself instead of finding fault with others."

A thought which comes from understanding and brings development and brightens the life is better than a thought that comes from misunderstanding which causes obstruction and darkens the life.

God said in the Koran, "The noblest of you in the sight of God are the best in conduct."

If people have inner intelligence, they will never become angry. Whenever you get angry, you disturb the design of the cosmos. You send negative vibrations to the life and nature which are the perfection of God's work. There is a divine law that if a person transgresses it by being angry and complaining, God will punish him by making him more angry and more complaining. Anger and complaining are blasphemy against God.

People who get angry and complain will be punished by misery and horror. They deserve every little bit of it, because they ask for it. In the Middle East they say, "Each carcass hangs from its own leg." You can't hang one carcass of a sheep by the leg of another sheep. This means you are completely responsible for your own doing.

Invitation from Heaven

There is a magic in the Koran. If you grasp this magic, your life will be magical. This magical life will be a beautiful life. This beautiful life will be a ideal life. This ideal life will be a perfect life. A perfect life will make you perfect. When you are perfect, you will know the meaning of *Allah*.

The word *Allah* is the invisible key. The "*h,*" which is the last letter of *Allah,* is the invisible door to the invisible reality. When you learn how to use the key, the invisible door will open wide. God said in the Koran, "You will see what no eyes have ever seen and hear what no ears have ever heard."

This is the inner beauty of existence which is absolute harmony, joy and peace. People have been given a power which is very special and distinct from all the other creatures. Through their intelligence, they could discover miraculous things, if they use their intelligence according to the nature of intelligence.

If they respect their intelligence, they will soar high like an eagle in the sky. If they abuse their intelligence, they will be sinking into dark bars, into dark corners of misery and strife. Choice is the most valuable thing a human being has. It is like pearls in a sapphire basket on an emerald tray that is offered to a man. If he values and honors it, he will be happy. If he dishonors and throws it in the mud, his life will be muddy, dirty and unhappy.

The Enchanted Oasis of the Ringed Dove

Habits and conditions are of two kinds, one is good and the other is bad. Bad habits throw you out of balance and the real beauty of reality shrinks away from you. The existence becomes narrow and dark. Heaven and earth become constricted, stiff and on edge. They dwindle in your eyes. Your days become dark and your nights become darker. It is good to get rid of bad habits and to establish good habits.

Good habits are connected with the truth. The more good habits you have, the closer to the truth you will be. Good habits are simple and easy. For example, you should develop a taste for water and should not drink cola. You will be closer to God. It is simple, but it is true and it goes for anything in life. Nature, consciousness and life, if they could drink water and were given the choice between water and cola, they would choose water.

If you drink and are given the choice, you should choose water. You will be a friend and in good company with nature, consciousness and life. You will be filled with nature, consciousness and life. You will be bubbling with nature, consciousness and life. Life will be lovable and love will be lovable. Nature, consciousness and life will enter your heart and you will freely enter the domain of nature, consciousness and spirit. Your heart will be pure and filled with love. When the heart is pure, you will learn the language of purity. The purity of your heart will talk to the purity of heaven. You could invite heaven to be with you and heaven will invite you to be with heaven.

The Rain

The rain falls on the earth.
The rain makes the earth clean.
The rain makes the earth green.
The rain makes the earth pure.
The rain runs in the mountain.
The rain flows in the valley.
The rain makes the rivers —
rivers full of pure water.
Water makes waves.
Waves dance and shimmer in the light
of sun and moon.
The rain gives the earth colorful garments.
The rain makes the earth beautiful.
The rain is generous.
The rain gives the earth perfumed roses,
a gift from heaven to earth.

God said in the Koran, "Do we not send down from the clouds water in abundance that we may produce with it grain and vegetables and gardens of luxurious growth? Truly, for the righteous, there will be a fulfillment of the heart's desires."

The materialistic man of today thinks that he is civilized and has a lot of knowledge. But he pollutes the water and destroys nature and himself. He is unpleasantly and strikingly ignorant, not only of the real knowledge, but also of the knowledge of himself. He follows

The Enchanted Oasis of the Ringed Dove

his whims and desires and both of these come from darkness where there is no spirit. They will lead him to darkness and he will fall into a dark reality. Whether he is in a dark reality or about to fall into a dark reality, he is confused and falling to pieces. So to fall into the dark reality will be the final, lasting misery.

When there is no spirit, his thoughts come out like plastic toys and his actions are worse than that. Otherwise, he would not destroy the beauty of nature and the planet. What this materialistic man needs is to find his spirit and to be in harmony with himself, his family, his friends, people, nature, the reality and to be at peace with peace and to fill his heart with tranquility and contentment.

The word for contentment in Arabic is *ridha,* which is the highest development in spiritual attainment. When you get to the highest and finest level of it, then everything becomes positive and has the assurance of the knowledge of the heart. The knowledge of the heart is sustained by the spirit. The spirit makes no mistakes. The spirit is sustained by a greater spirit which encompasses all that exists in the entire existence. If you are nowhere near that, then you are in complete darkness. But if you are near it or in it, you do not need to be reminded.

Ghazzali said, "He who tastes will know." It is that simple. If you have never tasted pickled pig's knuckles, have a bite and you will know.

The Emperor and the Pickled Pig's Knuckles

Pickled pig's knuckles were forbidden in Judaism, Christianity and Islam and they are still forbidden in Judaism, Christianity and Islam. But the law became loose in Christianity because a Roman emperor used to love eating pickled pig's knuckles for a gourmet dinner. He could not imagine having to give up this delicacy. So, he said he dreamed that the prohibition against pickled pig's knuckles had been lifted and now it was okay to eat, feast and indulge in eating pickled pig's knuckles. You could even vomit and eat it again and you could do that all night. In the morning, you don't need to work, you could take the day off. This was by the order of the emperor who was also considered a god, therefore, he could change whatever he didn't like. He did this so everyone would love him.

Ghazzali said, "A man may slip and stumble. It is as true as it is inevitable with one encompassed by human infirmity."

The emperor was a shrewd politician besides being an emperor and a god. He always used to say, "A god must take care of his people. And all the people are my children. I give them a lot of holidays so they will give me a lot of eggs and chicken and chickens and eggs. Eggs and chickens are truly my weakness. I could eat chicken cacciatore anytime, day or night, night or day. I never miss the midnight snack. Of course, my midnight snack is a banquet that continues to the light of the dawn."

Two Kinds of Contentment

When you get to the highest and finest level of contentment, everything becomes positive and has the assurance of the knowledge of the heart. You are on the top of the world. Contentment has many levels, like a sea. It starts shallow at the shore and goes deep.

Contentment is of two kinds. One is a contentment that fulfills the desires, whims, ego and negative self.

The Enchanted Oasis of the Ringed Dove

This contentment culminates, in the end, in sorrow and suffering. It is a temporary and quick pleasure which is not real. It is connected with the senses, the passions and emotions in a raw state.

This kind of contentment belongs to the materialistic consumer and technical society. It also belongs to the weak, the sick, the destitute and to people who have neither will, discipline, perceptions, awareness nor intelligence and to people who are lovers of cake, cola and all the mish mash gooey junk foods that brings poison to the body and mind and causes the sickest looking vibration to radiate from their faces. They cannot see it, though, because of the pollution that has filled their bodies. They assume a desperate, weak existence and cannot comprehend or apprehend anything positive.

Mentally they operate at a low key as if they are under cover and can barely communicate. Their main communications deal with trivial, futile, meaningless subjects, because their minds cannot see beyond the cake and the plastic duck which sits in the tub to commemorate her pal, the walky talky plastic man, who abuses himself and consumes his spirit with liquor, nicotine, caffeine, negative thinking and is a slave to the whims of the ego.

The Spirit in the Glass

The irony of the matter is that materialistic man has no spirit to start with. That is why he made friends with the plastic duck, Quack Quack. What makes it even worse is that he doesn't put any effort into finding out what spirit is. All he knows is that he has spirit in his glass and it makes no sense to him to look for spirit outside the glass. The spirit in the glass is right under his nose and he can smell it. Outside the glass, he smells no spirit.

"Therefore," he concludes, "there is no other spirit outside of the glass. There is nothing but space. Where the space goes nobody knows. I am not going to run after spirit when nobody knows where it goes. The only other place where there is spirit is in bottles.

"So, I am pleased, content, happy and extremely rejuvenated with the utmost pleasure when I look in the glass and see that my spirit is there. My lips twitch and quiver when I look at my spirit in the glass which has a golden rim. It is a special china glass.

"It was love from the first taste when my lips felt the tingle of wine when they touched the golden rim of the china glass. I breathed in the smell, too and became intoxicated. The inside of me started to quiver and dance and I felt as if I were Salome who loved Ya'hiyah, John the Baptist. But he didn't love her and then she wanted his head."

Zakareeyah, Mary and John the Baptist

The meaning of the name Ya'hiyah is "to live" and is connected with the story of the father of Ya'hiyah. His name was Zakareeyah. He was an old man and his wife was also old and they had never had a child.

Zakareeyah was the guardian of Mariam (Mary) and used to visit her in her sanctuary where she prayed. He saw that she had a lot of fruits of different seasons of the year and he asked her, "Mary, how did you get these?"

Mary said, "It is from God."

This would happen again and again. This inspired Zakareeyah to ask God to give him a son, to keep the line

The Enchanted Oasis of the Ringed Dove

of the prophet going. God fulfilled his desire. God told Zakareeyah that he would have a son named Ya'hiyah.

Now if Zakareeyah had been negative, tense and confused, God would not have give him a son and would never have look him in the face. But Zakareeyah was a very devout and very contented man. His spirit was rich and his disposition, very pleasant. His contentment was always enriched by his spirit. It was a real contentment that comes from the spirit. It was true and not phony.

Phony contentment leads people to a deep ignorance of spirit and real love. This phony contentment is ephemeral and overwhelms the conscience when the conscience is weak. The negative self withdraws when the conscience is strong and awake.

The Rabbit and the Fountain Pen

The other contentment is the contentment of spirit. It is usually difficult to know, because when there is no spirit, there is nothing to know. It is like giving a pen to a rabbit and saying to the rabbit, "Write the word 'rabbit.'" You could say that over and over again, but the rabbit is in a reality completely different from human reality and there is no connection whatsoever between the two.

One reality seeks a higher and better perfection in the intelligence. The other reality has no concern for intelligence except in a very limited way, to use it for jumping and running from danger, enjoying grass, wiggling the tail and contemplating carrots and the belly.

As far as the rabbit is concerned, what you are saying has no place in the world of rabbits. Whether the pen has ink or no ink does not matter.

But a man is not a rabbit. He is equipped with faculties that are most unique and intelligence without comparison and perceptions that are profound. What man has is a real miracle. Just think, a man can communicate through speech and express himself eloquently when he is not tense, negative and confused. Then, his voice will quiver and his words will blubber and what you hear will be a mumble and jumble.

Man has imagination, hope, expectation and dreams which make life a challenge and an adventure. Life is beautiful, charming and sweet. Every moment of it is pure magic. Enchantment is the depth of the inner reality. It is very possible to live it and to be in it, if a man simply would understand himself. But until that happens, man will be running in circles, not different at all from a mouse on a wheel.

When You Get the Attribute of the Wall

When a man is controlled by ego, the negative self, desires and phony contentment, he stands no chance and gets nowhere. He is running in the same spot on a pad or treadmill like they use in a gym to lose weight or on a stationary bike.

People think they are getting better from running on the treadmill or pedaling on the stationary bike. They might sweat, but all they get is anxiety and tension in their minds and their nervous systems. They would do better to ride a bike in a park or more pleasant surrounding where they can breathe good air and communicate with nature and the trees. Nature will suggest pleasant thoughts that inspire them to do good things instead of staring at the wall inside the gym where they are inspired to be gloomy.

The Enchanted Oasis of the Ringed Dove

There is a proverb in Arabic that says, "Tell me who you are with and I will tell you who you are."

So if you are with the wall and staring at the wall, the wall will stare back at you and you will get the attributes of the wall. You will finish your physical accomplishment as Mister Wall. You will say, "Hi Wally, I've come to ride my bike. Do you have anything to say or suggest to me?" The wall will subconsciously suggest to you to have a beer after practice and not to worry about gaining weight, because you are sweating a lot.

You should not worry about losing weight because you have already lost your life. What is left of your life is a shadowy, hectic existence that gets you nowhere.

The Bird and the Cage

You could pump all the liquor in the world into your belly, but you will never get happiness. Happiness is a bird which flew away and left you with an empty cage. The cage is your body and the bird is your spirit. And you could sing, "Bye, bye contentment. Bye, bye happiness. Hello emptiness, I think I'm an empty cage."

If a man uses his faculties, intelligence and perceptions, and these are assets that no other creature has, in the right direction, he will get all that he wants, even the spirit. But if the man abuses his intelligence, he will be a rabbit. A pen with ink or no ink does not exist in the world of rabbits.

If the rabbit were to give advice to a man, he would say, "Oh man, go eat carrots. If you don't find them, your second bet is grass."

If you acquire spirit, you will never know greed, selfishness, sorrow, suspicion or even the smell of these vicious collaborators whose sole purpose is to get you into the worst existence and to make you go through life without understanding the meaning of life or the pleasure of life or the harmony of life or the beauty of life, how delicate, deep and meaningful. If you have no spirit, you will know none of these things and will be miserable, complaining and rigid and your life will be sorrowful.

God gave you intelligence as the best thing that ever happened to you. If you have the right attitude and positive thought and refrain from any negative thought, your life will be beautiful.

Be a bird in flight. Go where there is pure air and clear sky.

ॐﻉ

Control your mind in a positive way and your thought will ride on a rosy float in a parade of joyous celebration accompanied by the smiles and laughter of the spectators. This is when your thoughts are beautiful, charming and lovable. The spectators will be applauding and shouting, 'Beautiful thoughts, teach us how to have beautiful thoughts like you.'